I0475186

My Time To Color

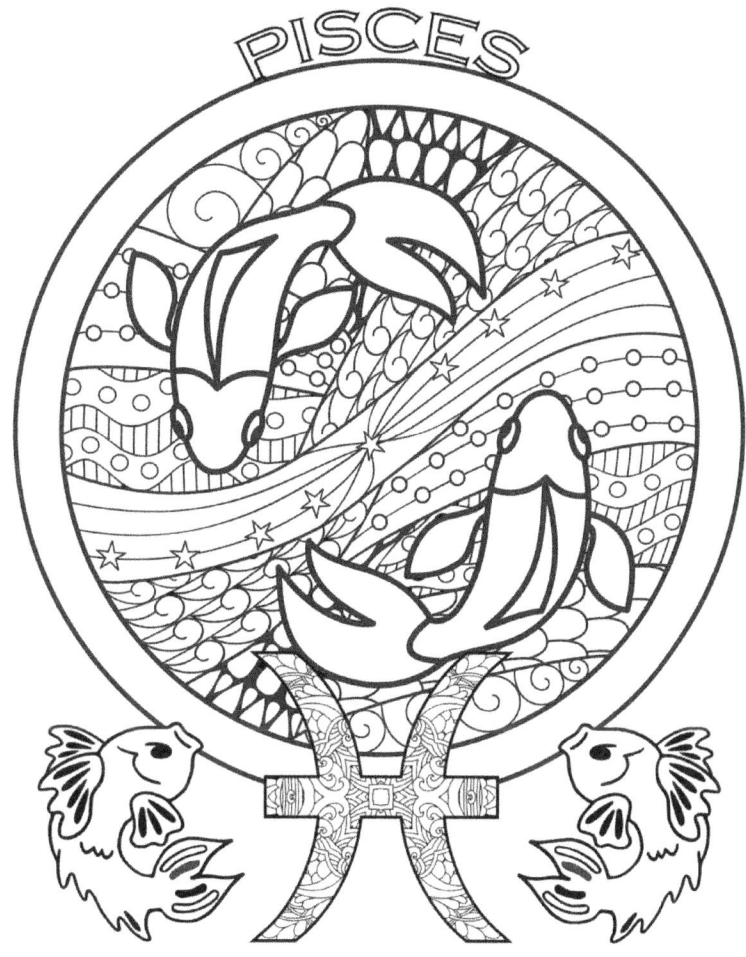

Pisces Zodiac Sign

Coloring Book

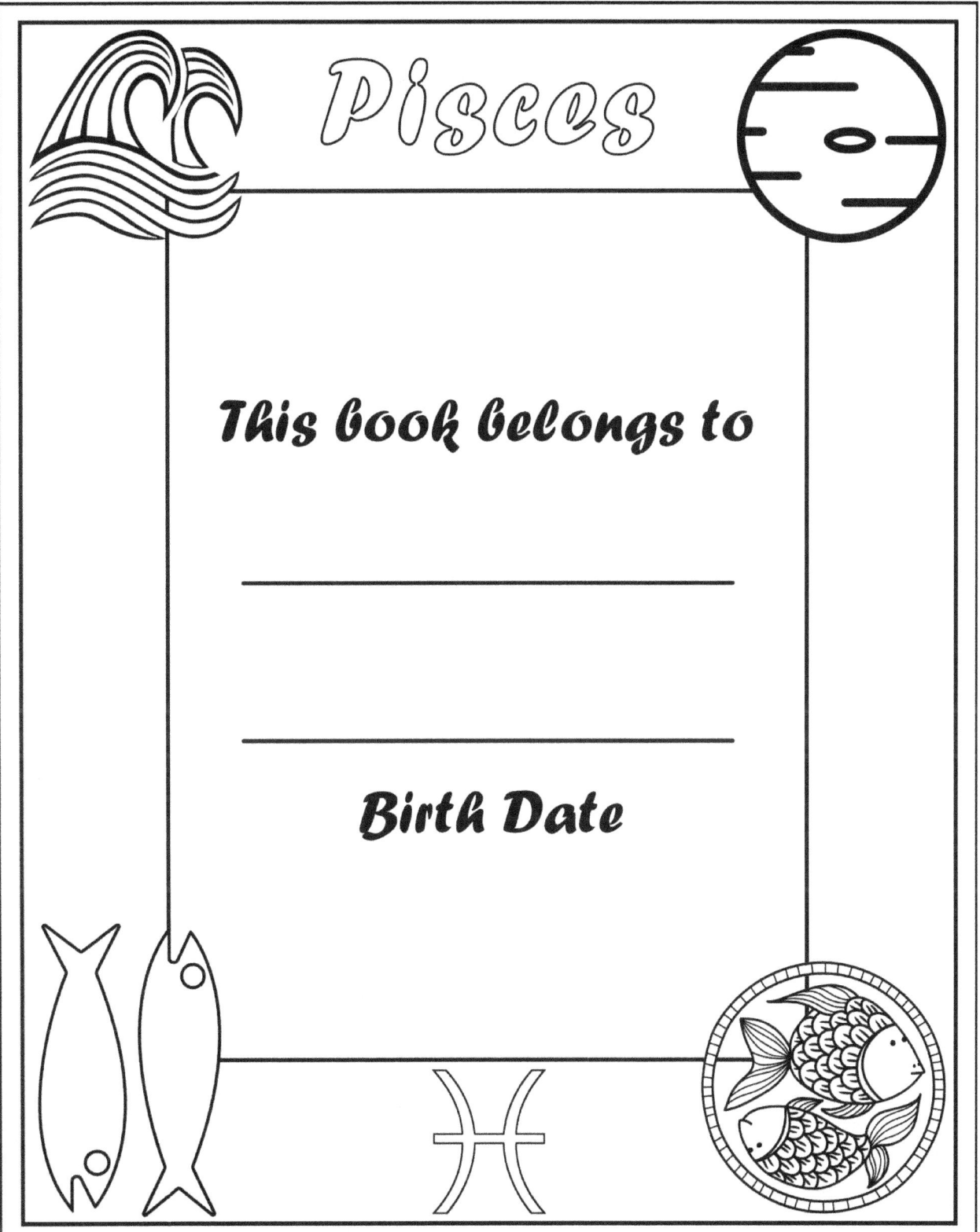

Pisces

This book belongs to

_____

_____

Birth Date

BORN ON THE CUSP?

Your zodiac sign is based upon the position of the Sun when you were born. At the time and place of your birth the Sun was in a specific position and therefore within a specific zodiac sign. While it would be more convenient if the Sun's transition from one sign to another happened exactly at midnight on any given day, it doesn't. Plus there are many various time zones throughout the world, so your midnight would not be the same as midnight for someone in a different time zone.

In addition, a calendar year is not the same as the Earth's annual revolution (circling) of the Sun. The actual length of a sidereal year (time required for Earth to revolve once around the Sun) is actually 365.25635 days. That is why every four years there is a leap year of 366 days to compensate for the error caused by the calendar year being shorter than the sidereal year.

This is why the Sun can be in different zodiac signs on the same calendar day in different years. The start and end dates of the zodiac signs can and do vary from year to year.

In reality the Sun was in one specific position, and therefore one specific sign, when you were born. Before the age of computers it used to be very time consuming to determine your sign if you were born on the cusp (near the beginning or end of a sign).

Now there are online calculators that you can use to make this determination. You will get the most accurate results if you have all three of these: 1) your day of birth 2) your time of birth and 3) your place of birth. Most calculators will still allow you to calculate your sun sign without your time of birth but the determination could be off. Input these three items into an accurate online sun sign calculator and you will be able to confidently determine your Sun sign.

This web page has an online calculator for determining your sign:
www.MyTimeToColor.com/sign

ZODIAC SUN SIGN PISCES

February 20 to March 20   (* see 'Born on the CUSP?')

Symbol: Fish

Element: Water

Quality: Mutable

Ruling Planet: Neptune

Lucky numbers: 3, 7

Color: Soft sea green

Favorite Environment: Seashores, Coastal cities

Governs: Feet, Liver and Lymphatics

Best Pet: Fish

Flowers: Orchid

WHAT IS ASTROLOGY?

Astrology is the use of heavenly bodies to guide us in our lives. It is based on the belief that the stars and planets have a direct impact on our lives and that their relative positions to each other predict certain events. Most people know astrology from their horoscopes and some characteristics of their Zodiac sign, but there is much more to it. You can gain a deeper knowledge of astrology and use it to improve your life.

There are twelve Zodiac signs. Your day and time of your birth determines your zodiac sign. Each Zodiac sign also has a quality, an element, and a ruling planet (or two). For example, if you were born November 14th, (like me!) your sign is Scorpio, your element is Water, your quality is Fixed, and your ruling planets are Pluto and Mars. Each of these pieces of astrological information give you useful knowledge about yourself and how you will interact with people of different Zodiac signs.

History of Astrology

Astrology has a rich history and has arisen independently in many civilizations throughout the centuries. Ever since the rise of humans, people have been observing the stars and planets. Knowledge of these bodies increased drastically with writing to record patterns that took place over long periods of time. Astrology first originated with the Babylonians about 4,000 years ago, when they began to use the stars to predict seasonal and astronomical events.

Since there are 12 lunar cycles in a year, they associated a constellation with each cycle, one that was always in the same part of the sky during that cycle. They then named these constellations after animals and gods. These constellations could be used to tell somewhat reliably what was about to happen with the weather, so we have the stars predicting the future. Astrology! They also believed that when a planet that represented a god gave bad omens, it meant that god was angry. They then attempted to appease it to protect the king and their nation, which meant they believed in a two-way interaction between the movements in the sky and the actions of humans.

The Chinese developed their own system of astrology, with twelve Zodiac signs based on animals representing the years in which they were born, and five elements. Confucius believed in astrology, saying, "Heaven sends down its good or evil symbols and wise men act accordingly." They believed that the stars and planets predicted the rise and fall of dynasties.

Astrology Brings Understanding

People today use astrology to understand their personality better and know what their strengths and weaknesses are. They can use horoscopes to know when there may be upcoming challenges or opportunities. Your response to your environment is determined by personality, and an important factor in your personality is your Zodiac sign and its corresponding quality and element. Therefore, astrology can explain how you will respond in certain situations. This understanding can be used to your advantage or, at the very least, help you to know that it's just the way you are.

For example, someone with the Fixed quality (Taurus, Leo, Scorpio, Aquarius) will often be uncomfortable in times of great change in their life. They could use this knowledge to realize why they are upset and then strive to regain a routine in life. Astrology offers certain psychological insights that are the accumulation of centuries of knowledge. These can be a powerful help in times of uncertainty.

It is important to remember to act decisively when faced with good fortune or looming catastrophe. The planets and stars will not live your life for you, however much they may influence your life. If you do not use the knowledge astrology provides, you have gained nothing.

Using Astrology in Personal Relationships

As it is a matter of great importance to many people, astrology has become highly refined in providing knowledge about significant others. Horoscopes often include advice or predictions involving your lover or crush. You can use your Zodiac sign in dating to have an idea ahead of time how a relationship would work with someone, based on their Zodiac sign and how yours interacts with it.

The relationship between two signs may be likely to work out because of shared interests and personality. Or it could be a cause for conflict, breeding misunderstanding and resentments. However, a good matchup between signs is no guarantee of a successful relationship, nor is a bad matchup a sure omen of a doomed one. Understanding your partner's astrological traits can help you to understand why your partner sees things and reacts to things the way they do. This can lead to more joyful times for both and it can help when working through conflicts. These sign interactions are a general guide to be used with consideration of other factors.

Astrology is helpful when it comes to interacting with your family. Understanding the characteristics of the signs for each of your family members can give insight on their words and deeds. You can learn about why there may be chronic conflict between two family members. You can use it to see an issue from the other point of view, which tends to decrease frustration and hostility. Reading horoscopes to family members can be a fun bonding activity.

For friends, astrology can be used to seek out the friendships most likely to succeed and to know why conflict arises and when that conflict may be irreconcilable, signaling it's time to move on. It can be used to understand the different mindsets of your friends and to know which ones would be best to undertake a project or go on a trip with.

Some signs have very different priorities and knowing and accepting the differences in your friend's motivations can be therapeutic. It can be very discouraging when you are excited about an idea and a friend shoots it down. It may be for a good reason, or it might be just because they have a different sign and mindset. In this case, it's best to share the idea with a friend of a more compatible sign.

ELEMENTS IN ASTROLOGY

The ancient Greeks believed that the world was composed of four elements: fire, earth, air, and water. Everything was a mixture of different amounts of these four elements. These four basic elements are no longer believed to be building blocks of our world, but they remain significant in astrology. In the same way that it was believed objects were composed of the four elements, it is now believed in astrology that the four elements make up our personalities. Each element has certain personality traits, and each sign has a unique mixture of these traits.

"China's Five Elements Philosophy" on chinahighlights.com explains that elements were first associated with zodiac signs in China in the Spring and Autumn period between 770 and 476 BC. Their zodiac signs are different animals, such as pig, rat, and dragon. They had five elements in traditional Chinese astrology: wood, water, earth, fire and metal. Each element was associated with 2 zodiac animals, except for Earth, which was attached to 4. As astrology spread from Asia and developed in Europe, each of the four ancient Greek elements became associated with 3 of the 12 zodiac signs.

Every person has an element, based on what their zodiac sign is.

The Air signs are Aquarius, Libra and Gemini.

The Water signs are Cancer, Pisces and Scorpio.

The Fire signs are Leo, Sagittarius and Aries.

The Earth signs are Capricorn, Virgo and Taurus

Your element affects you in many ways. It indicates certain personality traits that you have and explains how you will handle different situations. Your element is compatible with certain elements, so knowing your element can help you to find friends and lovers who are more likely to get along with you. Your element says a lot about what your strengths and weaknesses are and what kind of person you are. You can use this knowledge to play to your strengths and watch out for your weaknesses.

AIR

People whose sign is attached to the air element are intellectual; logical rather than emotional. They are witty, clever, and outgoing. They are excellent communicators because of their precise thinking. Because they are less reliant on emotion, they can remain calm and calculating in stressful situations.

They are most compatible with air, fire, and earth elements. They can have trouble with people of the water element because of the conflict between their calm logic and water's strong emotion. To bridge this gap, they need to speak the other's language, the language of feelings.

The heavy thinking that comes with the air element can be good or bad. With the Gemini, it causes indecisiveness due to over-analyzing things, but this prevents rash decisions. With the Aquarius, it means thinking about making things better far in the future, but this can cause their head to be in the clouds at times that require practicality. For the Libra, much of the thinking is about other people, but this can be expressed in either empathetic thoughts, or worrying about what other will think of them. Those with the air element would do well to remember that the world is not inside their head and that not everyone thinks as much as they do. However, their powers of intelligence are sure to serve them well in life.

WATER

Those whose sign connects with the water element are adaptable, emotional, and sensitive. They are deep and creative and they have great powers of imagination. They are in tune with the feelings of others and their observant qualities allow them to catch the subtle cues that a person in distress displays. They can be possessive and their knowledge of others emotions can be used for either nurture or manipulation.

The water element is most compatible with water and earth. For those of a water element dealing with people of the fire element, they should wear a thick skin and be ready to not take the fire element's occasional bursts of anger personally. They must remember that fire is impulsive and be patient with these people.

Those who are defined by the water element have strong emotions, and emotions can be powerful and difficult to control. However, emotion is a guiding force in our lives and shows us how to react to different circumstances.

A Cancer is loyal and very emotionally attached to their family, which is why it is good to be closely associated with a Cancer. A Cancer may overreact to perceived insults to their loved ones because they are so protective. The Pisces is friendly and altruistic, and rarely judgmental, but this faith in humanity may lead to them being taken advantage of, which causes many a Pisces to become depressed. Pisces are prone to sadness, but this also gives them an insight into the suffering of others, creating empathy with those in need. The Scorpio is brave and passionately attached to what they believe to be true. This can cause them to fight for something good, or if they are mistaken in their beliefs, to be a powerful force for evil. Their suspicious nature can protect them, but also make them paranoid, and therefore emotionally unstable.

Those with water as their element can overcome any weaknesses associated with emotionality by taking a time-out from the situation. A powerful emotion is like a strong fire, very hot, but quick to burn its fuel and end.

FIRE

Which brings us to the fire element! Those whose signs are attached to the fire element are energetic, impulsive, and enthusiastic. Their liveliness is inspiring and they make great leaders because of their charisma. They can also be very unpredictable and have a temper; they will be forceful when triggered. Adventurous and quick to try new things, people of the fire element are often groundbreakers and innovators. They stick with what their gut tells them and are very decisive.

Fire people are most compatible with air and fire people. When they deal with those of the earth element, they may become irritated with how grounded and practical they are and consider them boring. In this case, a fire person should keep their ego in check and realize that stable people are just as necessary as the impulsive ones.

The energy and charisma of people under the fire element can lead to a wide variety of outcomes. For the Aries, their energy is expressed in their speed and competitiveness. This impatience can lead to greatness, or frustration and anger. They always want to be first, and although they are very organized, their tendency to race through things can trip them up. For the Leo, their charisma leads to unparalleled leadership abilities. But they can also have a large ego and be stubborn and self-centered. Their ability to get their way from others means they might not address these issues, because they won't need to. When it comes to the Sagittarius, part of their charm is their uncompromising honesty. Their trustworthiness attracts people, but it can also drive them away if a Sagittarius says something brutally honest that hurts someone's feelings.

EARTH

The people whose sign is associated with the earth element can truly be described as down-to-earth. They are practical, emotionally stable, and reliable. They are not risk-takers nor are they prone to idealistic ambitions. Instead, they are focused on steadily making improvements in their lives and the lives of those they love. They are materialistic and intent on accumulating money and property.

Earth gets along best with earth and water. To get along with the fire element, earth people shouldn't try to save these impulsive risk-takers from failure, because they won't listen.

The stability and materialism of the earth element has predictable results. The Taurus is reliable yet stubborn and will be conservative in their life choices. They are good at making money, but they can also become greedy because of money's addictive properties. The Virgo does things systematically and never leaves anything undone. They are highly organized but this means they are prone to perfectionism. They can be judgmental of anyone who lacks their attention to detail, which may hurt someone's feelings. The Capricorn is disciplined and self-reliant. They are fond of tradition and value experience over experiment. Their commitment to tradition can lead to stubbornness and they often expect innovations to fail. Their faith in the tried and true can be utterly unshakeable.

ASTROLOGICAL QUALITY

In Astrology, there are 12 signs of the Zodiac. Each of these signs corresponds to one of three qualities: Cardinal, Fixed or Mutable. The qualities are also called quadruplicities because they each describe four of the Zodiac signs. Each quality has certain characteristics that correspond to the position in the season of the zodiac sign. The Zodiac signs that begin each season have the Cardinal quality, or "initiating energy". The Zodiac Signs in the middle of each season have the Fixed quality, or "maintaining energy". Finally, the Zodiac signs at the end of each season have the Mutable quality, or "changing energy".

Your quality says a lot about you and is an important addition to the self-knowledge astrology can provide. A person's quality determines both the inner energy of a person and how they respond to changes in their environment. It explains whether or not they are likely to change their opinions and how likely they are to be a leader or a follower. Knowing your quality can help you play to your strengths and realize what weak points in your energy you need to strengthen. Knowing where one needs improvement can be a path to greatness! Use this knowledge of qualities to achieve greater balance in your life.

Cardinal

At the beginning of each season are the four Zodiac signs with the Cardinal qualities: Aries, Cancer, Libra and Capricorn. These signs usher in the new season and get its momentum started up. Accordingly, people with the Cardinal quality love to start new things; they are innovators and trailblazers. They tend to be ambitious and energetic, eager to start new things. They seem to have endless drive towards accomplishing things, but they often don't finish what they start, because they get so excited about something new that they move on to that!

To go along with their ambition, those with the Cardinal quality can also have a large ego. A big ego is sometimes assumed to be a bad thing, but large egos come with confidence and the self-assuredness of leadership. They want to be the best at everything and work hard to get there. They are creative-types and innovators; trendsetters that the crowd will follow. However, they can be erratic due to their constant shifting of goals, and leaving things undone can cause problems.

Those with the Cardinal quality need to focus on finishing what they start. This may mean delaying a new project they are excited about in order to finish an older one. They can also surround themselves with people of the Fixed quality who will help them reach the finish line in all the races they start. It is very important that Cardinal quality people learn to finish their projects because of how valuable what they begin to create is!

Fixed

In the middle of each season are the four Zodiac signs with the Fixed quality: Leo, Taurus, Aquarius and Scorpio. If we compare those with the Cardinal quality to the hare who takes a nap because he is so far ahead in "The Tortoise and the Hare", we can say that those with the Fixed quality are like the tortoise. They prove that slow and steady wins the race. They have an innate ability to focus and stay committed. They are determined to reach their goals and will be persistent when faced with obstacles. People with the Fixed quality are the ones who get the job done, no matter how difficult or long the journey may be.

Fixed quality people prefer a predictable routine. Once they come to accept an idea or way of thinking, it is very hard or even impossible to get them to change their belief. This can be a strength, such as when they have an important moral belief that those around them have abandoned. It can also be a weakness when they refuse to adapt to new information. Fixed quality people are self-reliant but stubborn.

The best way for Fixed people to overcome their weakness is to open their mind and realize that they do not know everything. The entire universe is not already in their head and they need to be ready to accept new things. There is a Buddhist saying, "You cannot fill a cup that is already full." In this context, this means that when a Fixed person's mind is filled with beliefs that they won't let go of, there's no room to allow new beliefs to come in. Anyone with the Fixed quality should welcome the experience of being proven wrong and take advantage of the opportunity for growth that it offers.

Mutable

At the end of each season are the four Zodiac signs with the Mutable quality: Gemini, Virgo, Sagittarius and Pisces. These signs come at the end of the season, when weather is changing to make way for the new season. That's why the Mutable quality is the quality of change and adaptation. People who are Mutable are quick to follow the crowd and adapt to changes in their environment. This adaptability is extremely important for times of radical change; while those who are stuck in their ways are having problems, the Mutable people will already be back in stride.

Mutable quality people can be shallow, with no deep attachments to any principle, idea or way of life. This can be useful, as some people allow their beliefs to prevent them from seizing an advantage. Being opportunistic and flip-flopping has gotten plenty people ahead in life. However, doing so might get a Mutable person called out on their lack of commitment to ideals which others take very seriously. If they get caught acting different ways with different people, they will lose trust and rumors may spread.

The best way for Mutable people to make up for this weakness is to think for themselves. It's no shame to have other people's thoughts in one's head and be strongly influenced by trends; absolutely none of us are original in everything we think and say. However, the Mutable quality people need to find some time to be on their own and then decide what they think. Then they should take this out into the world and stick with it. No matter what your beliefs are, not everyone will agree with them, and that's okay. Not everyone has to be like you, or even like you!

RULING PLANETS: PISCES

Every Zodiac sign has a ruling planet. The planets are large bodies orbiting the Sun and in astrology they are believed to strongly affect the lives of humans on Earth. The exact scientific definition of "planet" differs from astrology's. For astrology, the moon and the sun are considered planets because they are large bodies in our solar system. The planets alter our destiny and interpreting their movements is one of the main functions of astrology. The position of the ruling planet for your Zodiac sign is a major part of determining your horoscope.

Where do ruling planets come from?

The idea that ruling planets are associated with people born at certain times originated with the Romans. They divided the calendar year into portions associated with heavenly bodies. The Earth was once thought to be the center of the universe. So, when the planets moved backwards and forwards in the sky, or moved faster or slower, they didn't understand that it was because of the Earth's movement. They thought the planets were trying to communicate with humans. The same way observations of the stars predicted the seasons, they thought movements of planets predicted human destiny.

Eventually, Zodiac signs began to be associated with certain months, which led to the ruling planets for months turning into the ruling planets for Zodiac signs. Some signs share a ruling planet with another sign and some signs have two ruling planets, a new one and a classic one. Signs like Pisces have two ruling planets (Neptune and Jupiter) because for ancient astrologers, the furthest planet that they knew of was Jupiter. When new planets were discovered, astrologers came to a consensus that some signs would be assigned to the newly discovered planets: Uranus, Neptune and Pluto. Their previous ruling planets are also considered significant, so these signs have two ruling planets.

The modern ruling planet for Pisces is Neptune. Neptune was the god of the sea, which is why it rules the fish sign Pisces. Like the sea, those ruled by Neptune are deep and mysterious. They are very in tune with unseen and mystical forces, and are far more likely to have psychic abilities. Neptune is the planet of illusions, which is why it's connected to acting, treachery and even self-deception. People ruled by Neptune can have trouble seeing things as they really are and since Pisceans have such a strong imagination, they can become disconnected from reality.

Neptune's influence encourages emotional sensitivity and helps break down the ego barrier between us and others. This explains Pisces' caring nature and desire to help the suffering. It also explains Pisces' moodiness and their recurring troubles coping with the strength of their emotions. The lack of focus on the self opens the mind up for creativity and dreaming. Those ruled by Neptune are free-thinkers and aren't restricted by the tunnel vision of ambition.

Neptune can bring us away from the everyday material world, into the realm of spirit and mind. Our lives are often ruled by routine, but Neptune can help us see opportunities for change by expanding our minds. Those ruled by Neptune will find that their spirituality constantly opens new paths for them and they would be wise to maintain a strong spiritual life. Embrace the unknown and life will become much richer.

The ancient ruling planet for Pisces is Jupiter. Neptune is more influential on Pisces, although some Pisceans can have more of the characteristics connected to Jupiter. Jupiter represents large spaces, grandeur, abstract thought, and learning. People ruled by Jupiter dream big and enjoy traveling to distant destinations. Jupiter's influence is associated with forcefulness, good judgment and philosophy. Jupiter rules over law and order, and those ruled by it will be lawful, decent, and honest; fair in all their dealings with others.

Jupiter is a magnifying power and accordingly, those ruled by it often have intense emotions and a greater vision of reality. Thus, Pisceans are open-minded, understanding that the world is not so simple that it can be explained in one way.

People ruled by Jupiter have a deep understanding of philosophy and always seek to increase their knowledge. Exploring new places is an important part of this! Travel broadens the mind and Jupiter encourages us to witness for ourselves how large our planet is. Jupiter allows us to go above and beyond ourselves, to experience much more than our small corner of the world.

Jupiter can help us connect with the cosmos and get in tune with the larger forces that control our universe. Divinity is more accessible than it may seem, but we must not wall ourselves off from it by swimming against the tide. Being ruled by Jupiter can bring great luck, sometimes beyond our wildest dreams. But this depends upon our ability to let go of our ego and experience joy independent of any personal gain. When we do not feel as though we need, we are most likely to receive.

SUN SIGN PISCES

The Pisces is a dreamer, very empathetic and artistic, but not very worldly. Pisces is a Water sign with the Mutable quality. Romantically, they get along best with Cancer, Scorpio, and Virgo, and have trouble with Sagittarius and Libra. Pisceans are emotionally complex individuals with vivid imaginations. They are open-minded, but easily influenced by others. Pisces is one of the most caring signs, though, and many of the kindest individuals have Pisces as their sun sign.

Pisces is a Water sign

Sun signs with Water as their element are emotional, empathetic, and adaptable. A Pisces is very in tune with the moods of those around them and is unable to ignore the distress of others. That's why they are so caring; because they are acutely aware of the emotions of others. For a Pisces to feel good, others around them must as well. They have a strong drive to care for the sick, sad and suffering.

This sensitivity has a downside: Pisces is easily influenced by others. This puts them at risk of being manipulated by people who are willing to fake emotions. Pisces may also identify too strongly with someone in pain and suffer because of it. This may be noble, but in certain situations it's much wiser to be selfish. Pisces worries too much about hurting others feelings, sometimes to the point of ignoring their own.

Pisces experiences very strong emotions and experiences life deeply. They are prone to extremes and drama. Pisces is at the whim of a powerful ability to feel and this can be overwhelming. To some it may seem like Pisces overreacts, but this is because their emotional abilities are not as strongly developed. Pisces often struggles with inner conflict that no one else can see.

Pisces is very artistic and they are dreamers. They tend to be mystical and otherworldly and have strong psychic abilities. Pisces can be both escapist and visionary. Their imagination can allow them to become writers, artists, and innovators, or it can cause them to live in an ideal dream world, where they choose to believe what makes them feel best.

Pisces has a Mutable nature

Pisces is known for being open-minded and adaptable, in keeping with its Mutable nature. A Pisces can thrive in many circumstances, because they tend to be like mirrors, reflecting those who surround them. A Pisces can fit in well with a group, but perhaps to a fault, because they can lose their identity. They go with the flow and change with the times. Since their character is more fluid than solid, they may hide from a difficult situation rather than confront it.

A Pisces is open to new ideas and can change the way they think with ease. This lack of attachment to specific ideas frees them to be creative and learn something from all kinds of people. Pisces will be well-rounded spiritually, because they are open to many spiritual ideas. They are less likely to adhere to dogma, yet more likely to be profoundly religious.

Pisces can display a laziness and indifference to their station in life. Because they adapt so well, it is not always important to them to find a good position. However, they may still struggle with sadness because they haven't fulfilled their potential. This is one of the reasons Pisces often struggles with alcoholism and drug addiction.

Best Matches for Pisces

Cancer is the best match for Pisces, because Pisces requires someone nurturing to help them have structure to their life and Cancer is solid, dependable, and protective of their loved ones. They both have sympathetic personalities and will care for each other well. Imaginative and artistic Pisces will delight Cancer, who can help Pisces put some of their ideas in action. Cancer is an Earth sign and will help Pisces in many ways with practicality and routine and be a positive influence on them.

Scorpio is a great match for Pisces, because Pisces is a born follower, and Scorpio loves to lead. Their roles complement each other and they make a great team.

They are both very emotional and passionate and their powerful mutual attraction will forge a strong bond. Scorpio and Pisces share an interest in mystical or unusual things and can enjoy things together that their former partners may have thought were weird.

Virgo is a good match for Pisces because of Virgo's great ability for communication. Pisces' fluctuating emotional states are sometimes hard to understand, but Virgo has a Mutable nature like Pisces. They can adapt to and accept Pisces' moods, then talk to them about their feelings better than others could. Virgo is often busy and their hard work will set a good example for Pisces.

Worst Matches for Pisces

The worst match for a Pisces is a Sagittarius. Pisces is very sensitive and requires devotion and romance to sustain their feelings of love. Sagittarius is a free spirit and easy-going and will not want to be too tied down, which may make the Pisces feel unwanted. Sagittarius can be careless with their words, and may hurt Pisces deeply without even meaning to do so. Though they may be great for others, Sagittarius is not the one to provide the thoughtful nurturing the Pisces requires. They will have trouble developing a deep emotional connection and the relationship may not last long.

Libra can be a bad match for Pisces. Things will likely start off great, but there are fundamental flaws that will become apparent once the "honeymoon" effect wears off. First, Libra is very social and enjoys parties and large gatherings, whereas Pisces likes solitude and staying home alone. This is a recipe for disaster when they live together, because Libra may want to have people over all the time and Pisces won't be able to get any peace. Most Libras don't have the patience necessary to deal with Pisces' sensitive nature, and will become frustrated when Pisces most needs their support.

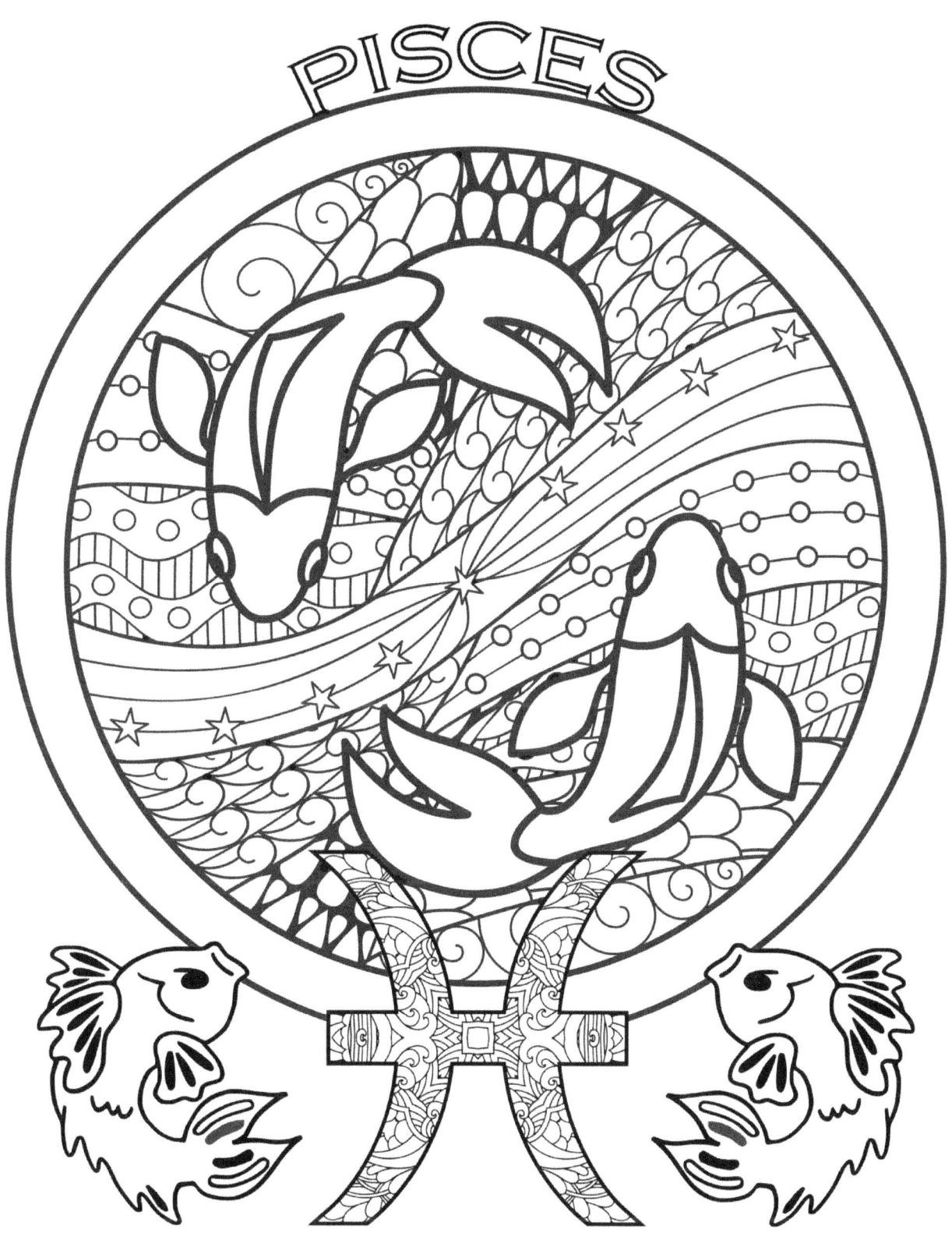

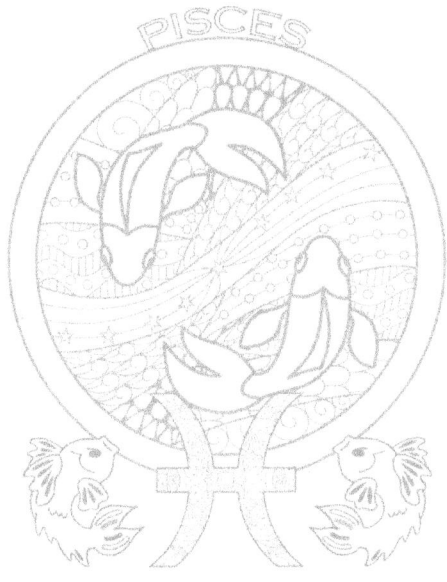

Pisces' ruling planet Neptune brings you away from the everyday material world, into the realm of spirit and mind. Pisces loves dreaming to connect to this realm.

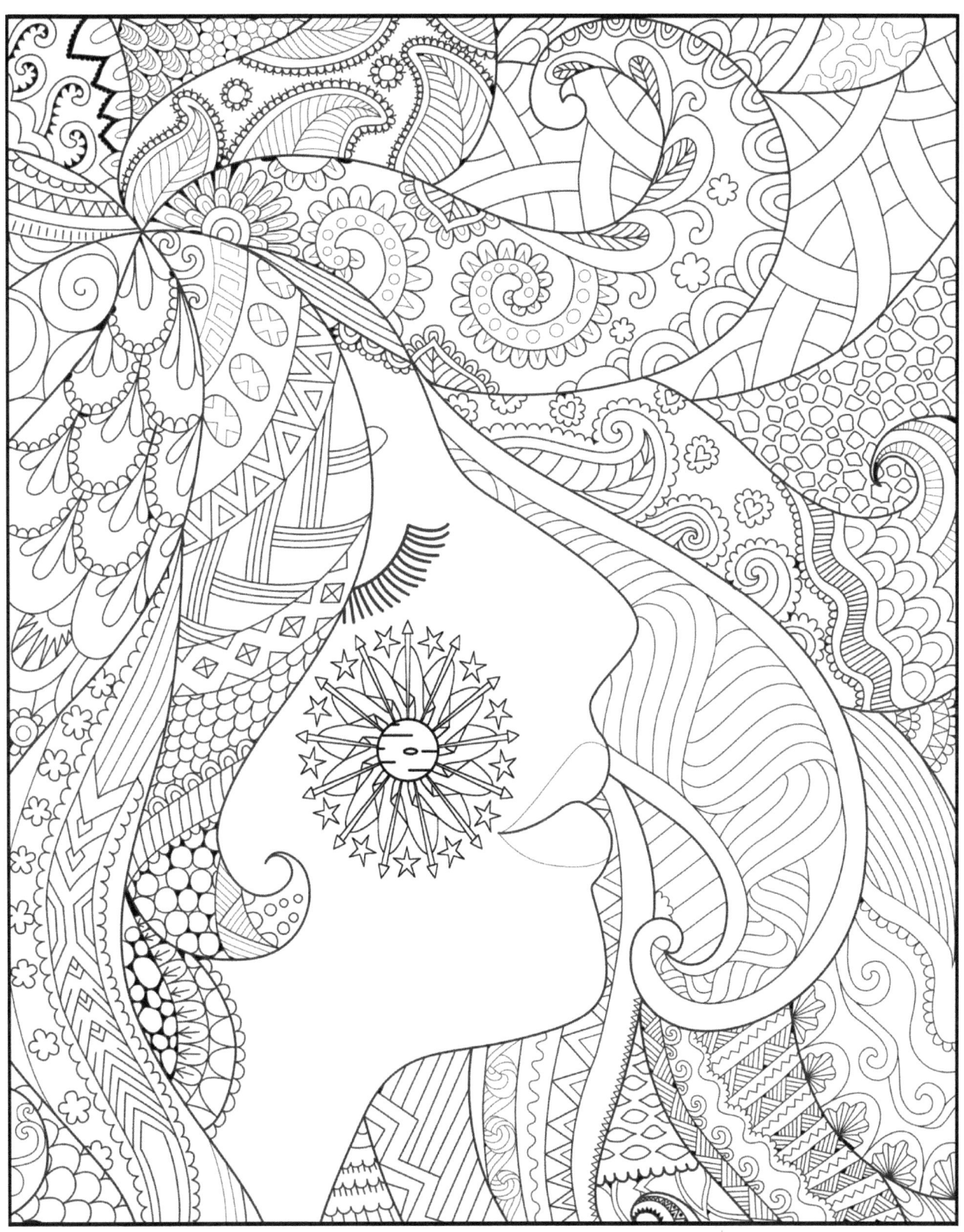

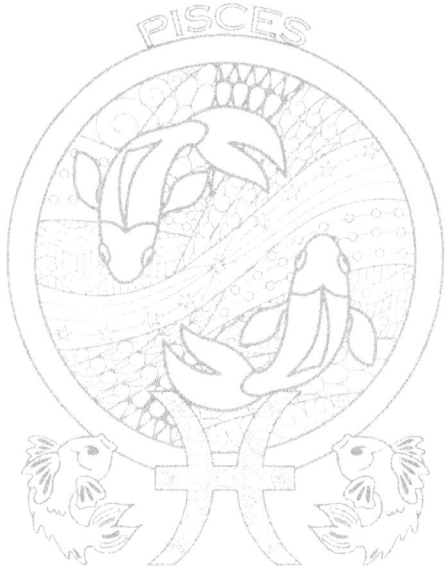

Being lovers of water and fantasy can give the Pisces a strong affinity for this legendary aquatic creature, the mermaid.

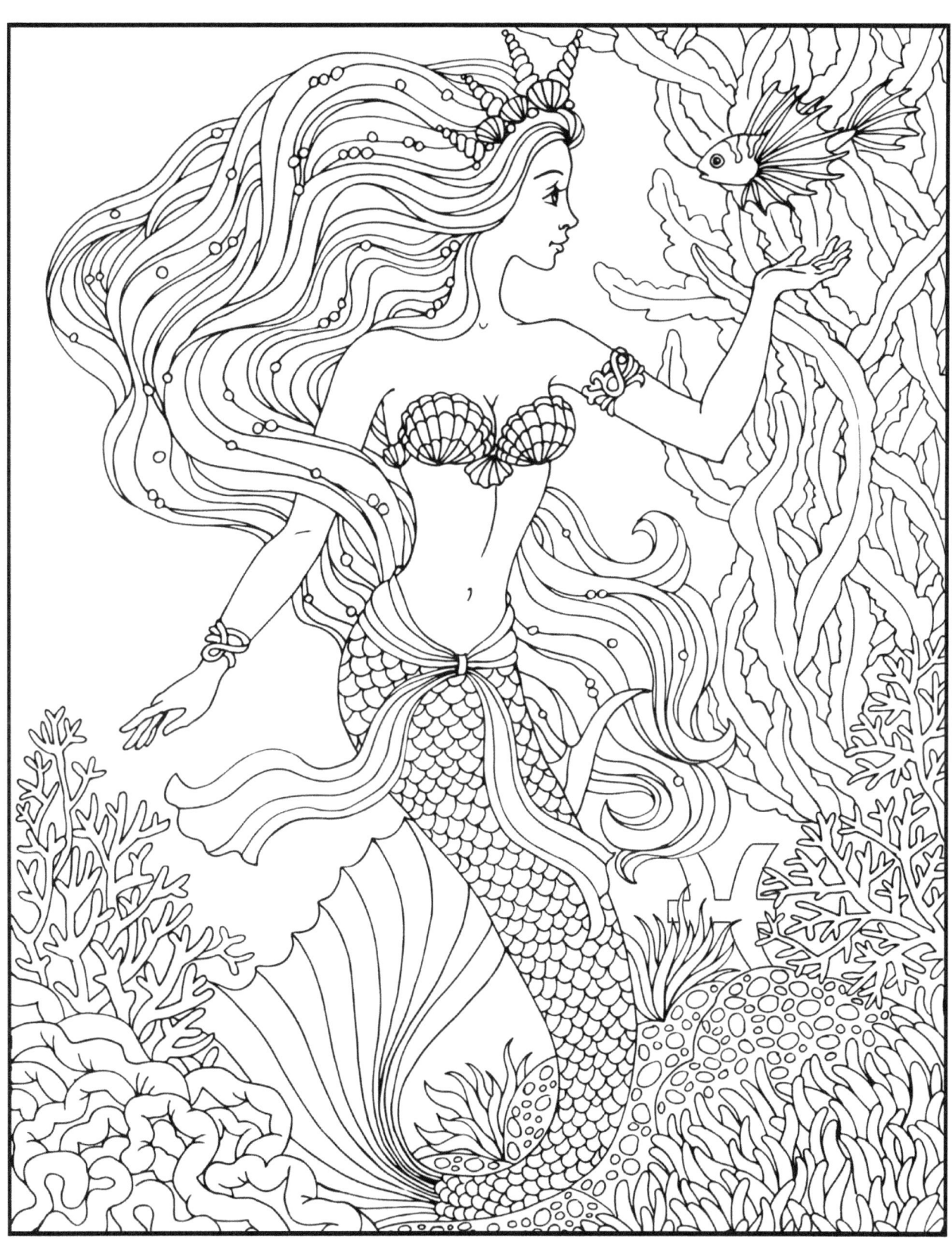

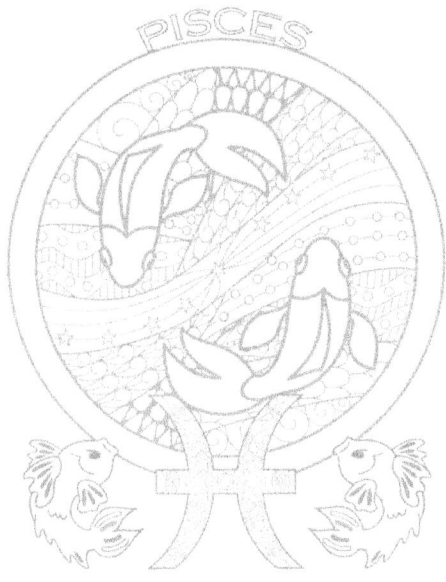

Musical and artistic talents are strong within Pisces.

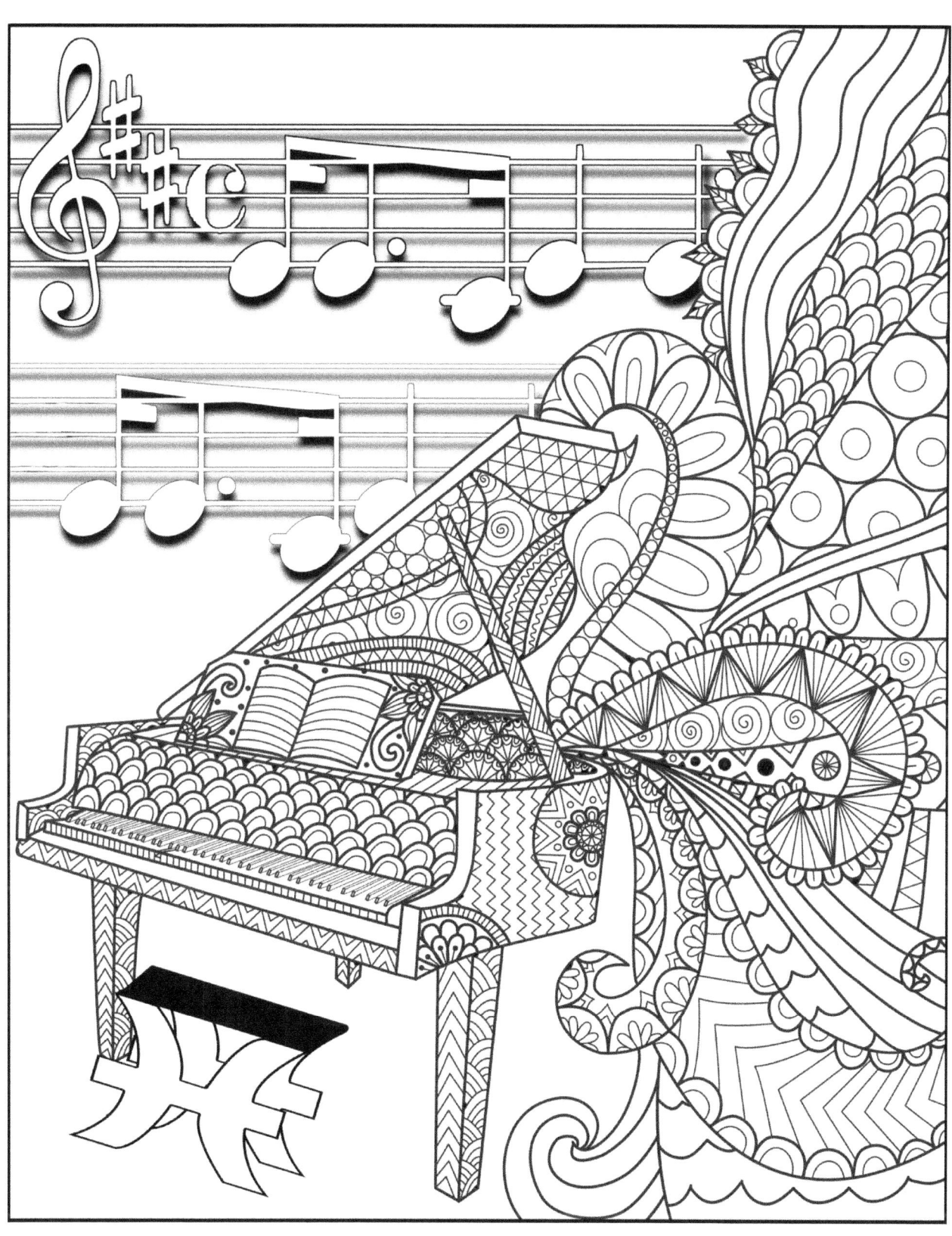

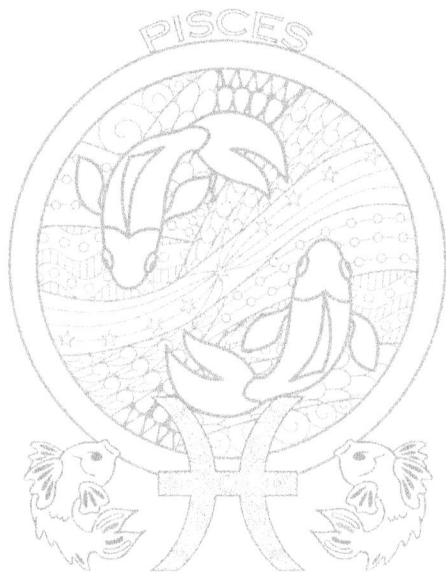

Fish, especially Koi, can be a perfect pet for Pisces. They can also be a great tattoo.

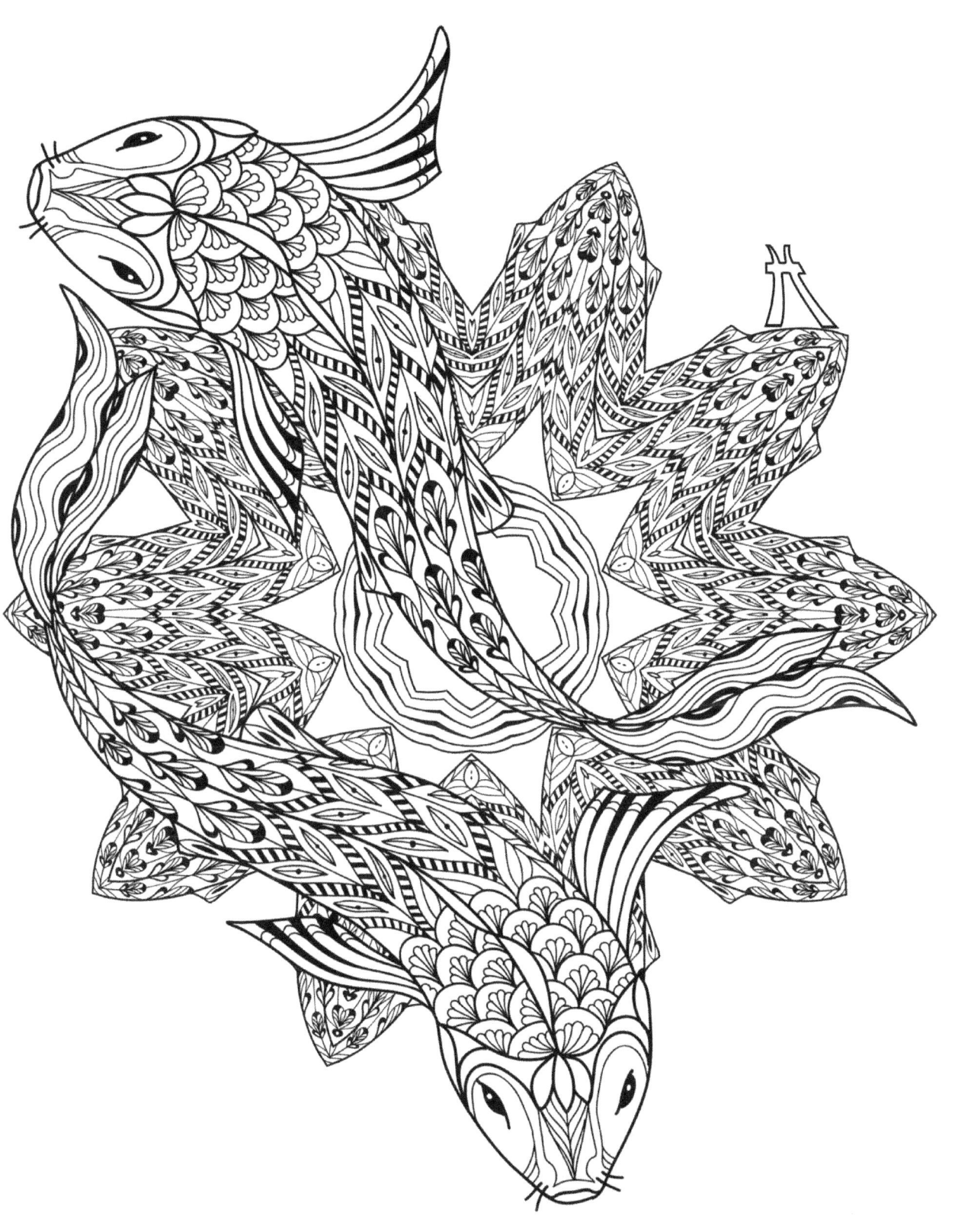

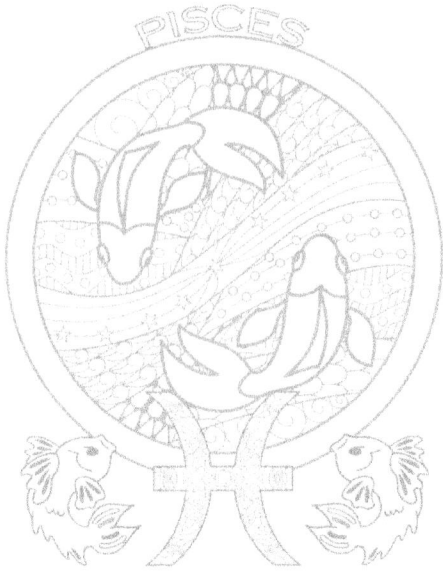

Neptune is the planet of illusions and Pisces loves fantasies.

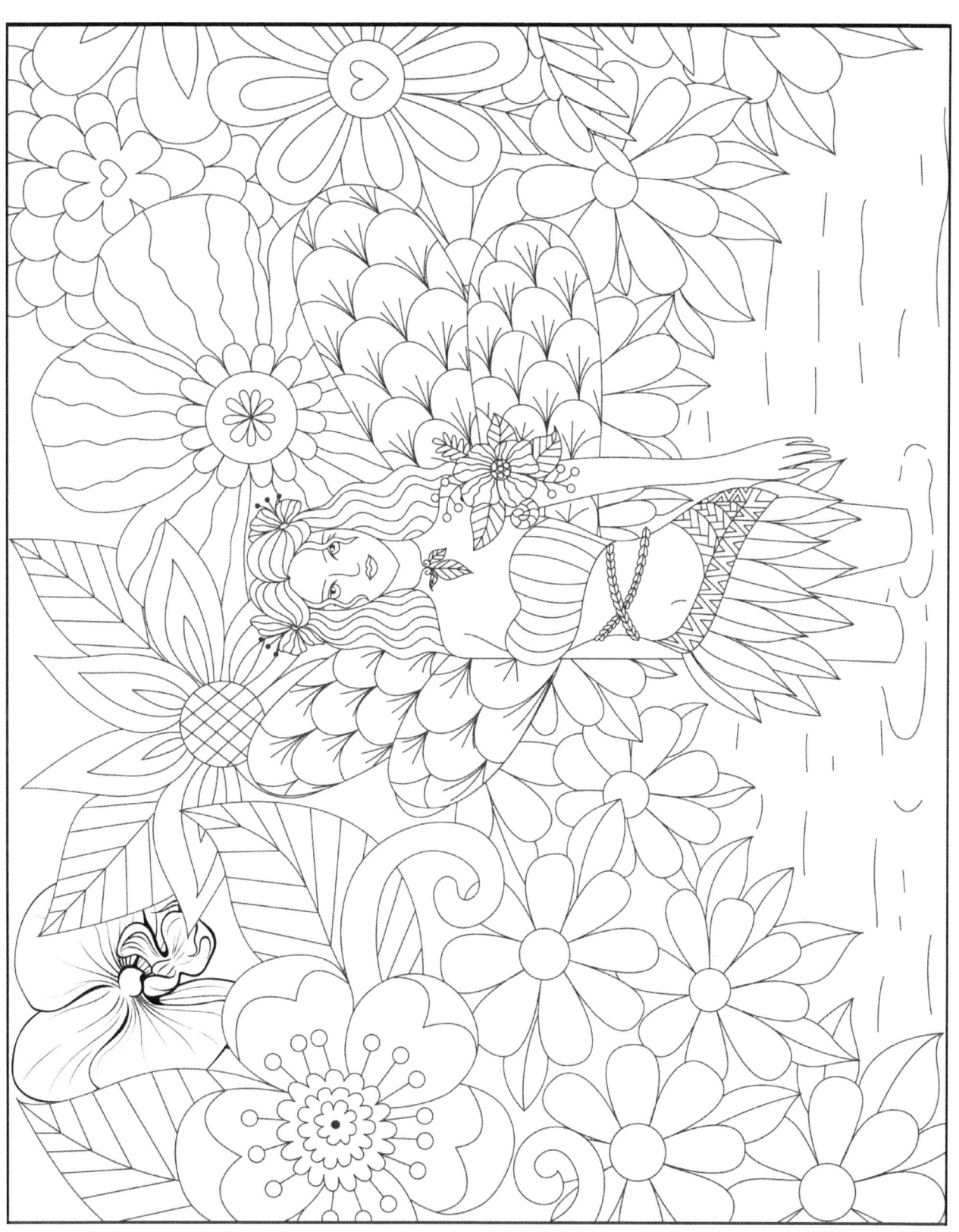

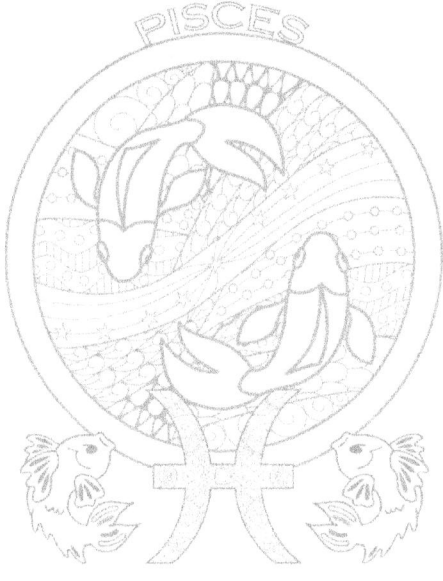

It has been said that there are two types of Pisces in the world; fish and whales.

_____

_____

_____

_____

_____

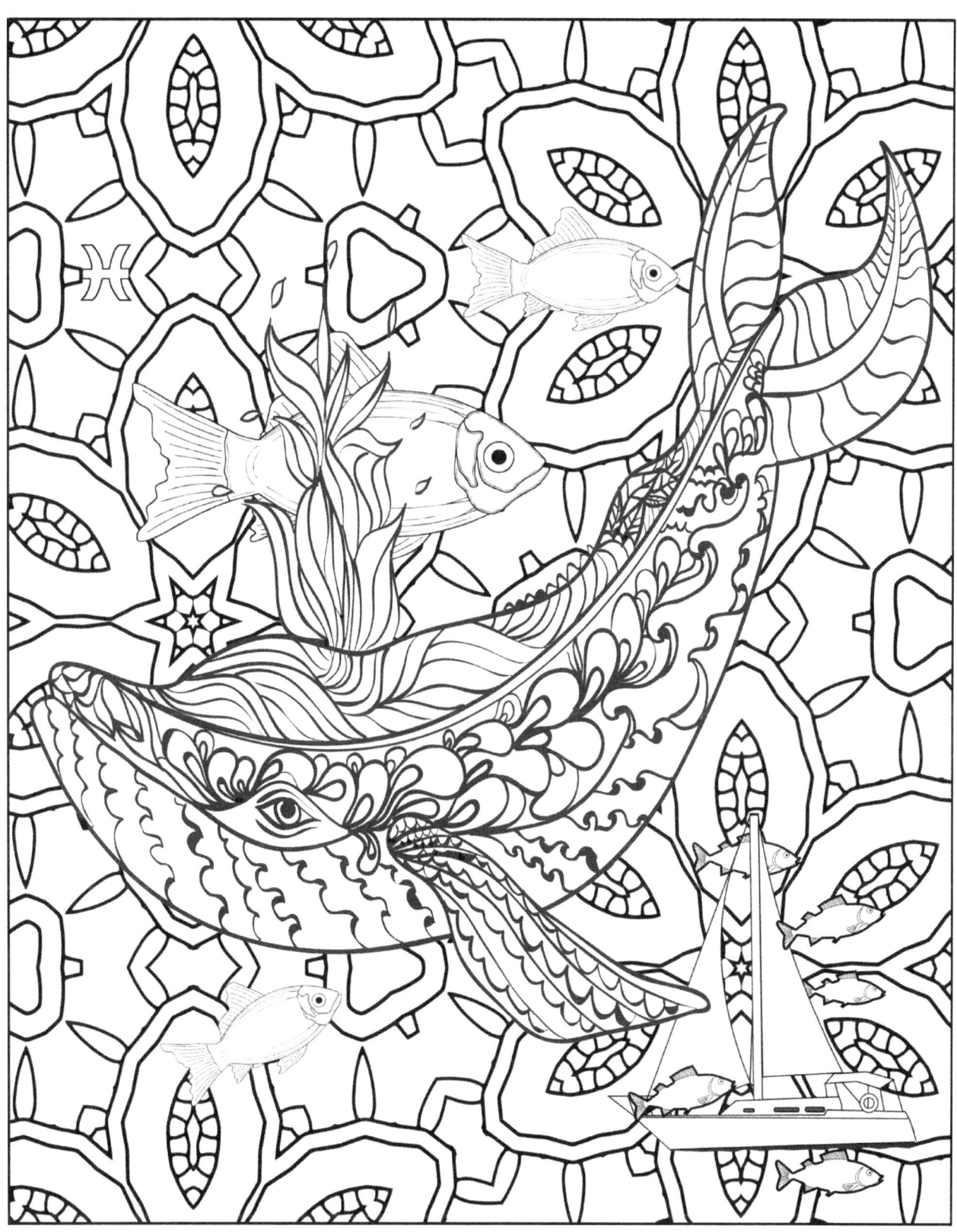

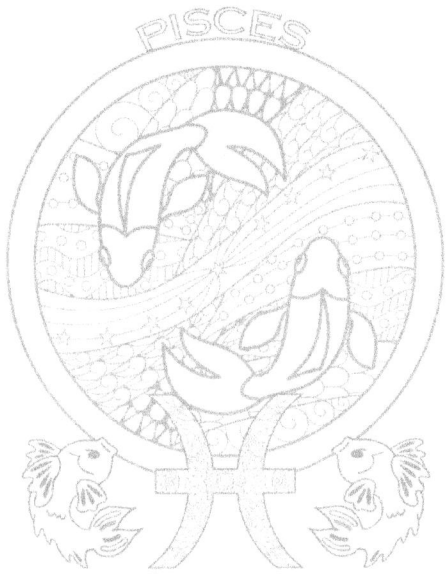

Pisceans are fascinated by anything that offers an enhanced connection to the Earth and the otherworlds. Yoga can be a great way to make these connections.

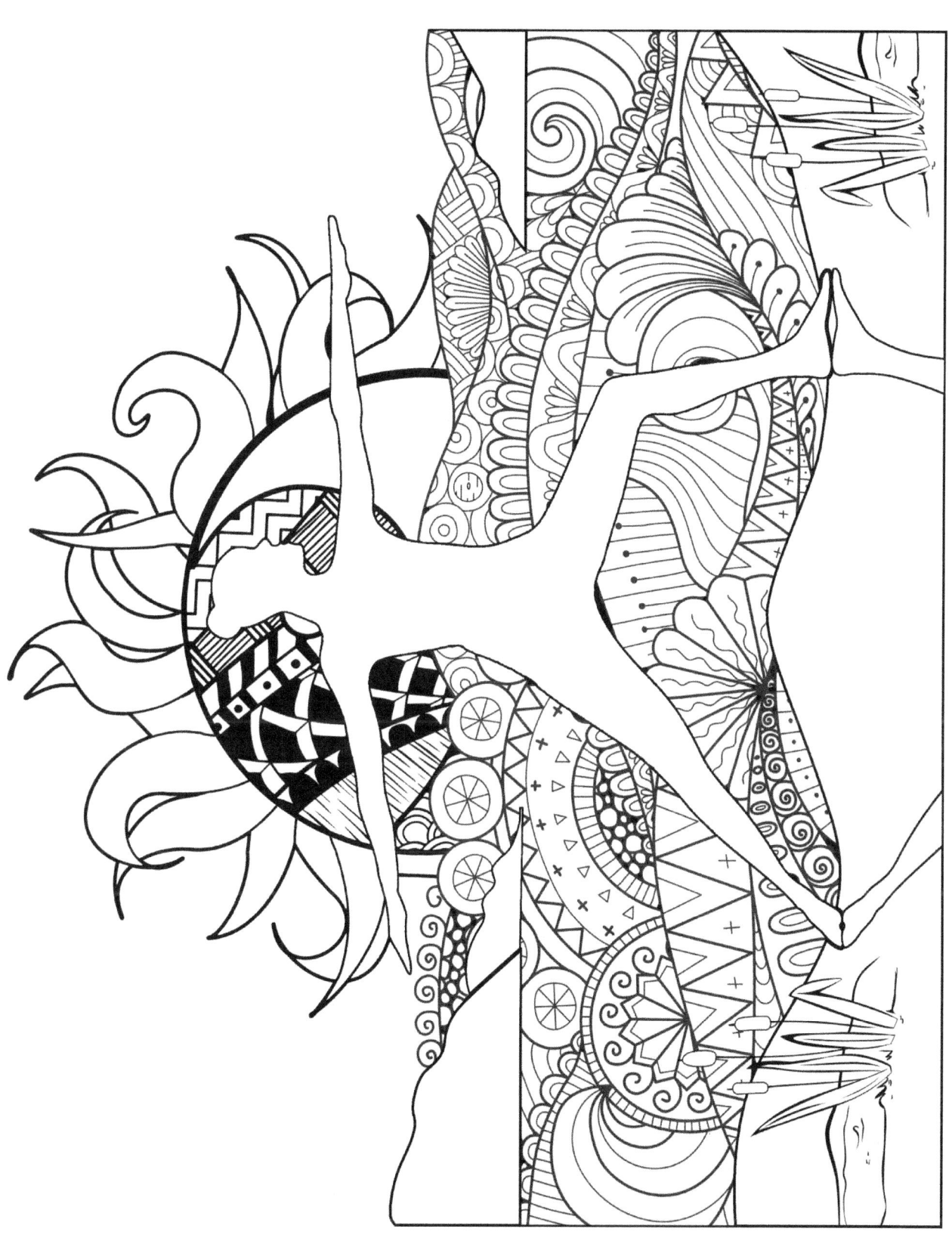

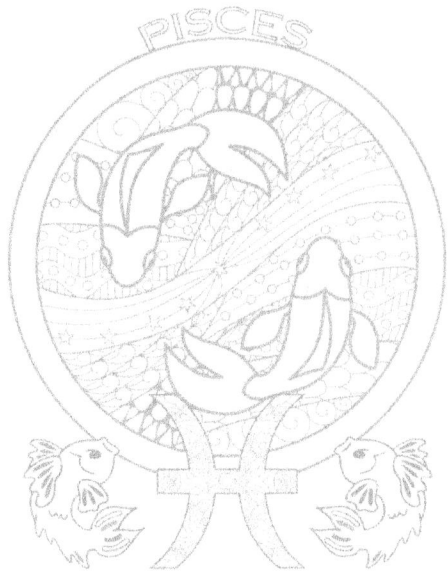

True to their element, most Pisces individuals are found to enjoy water related sports and activities like the beach and surfing.

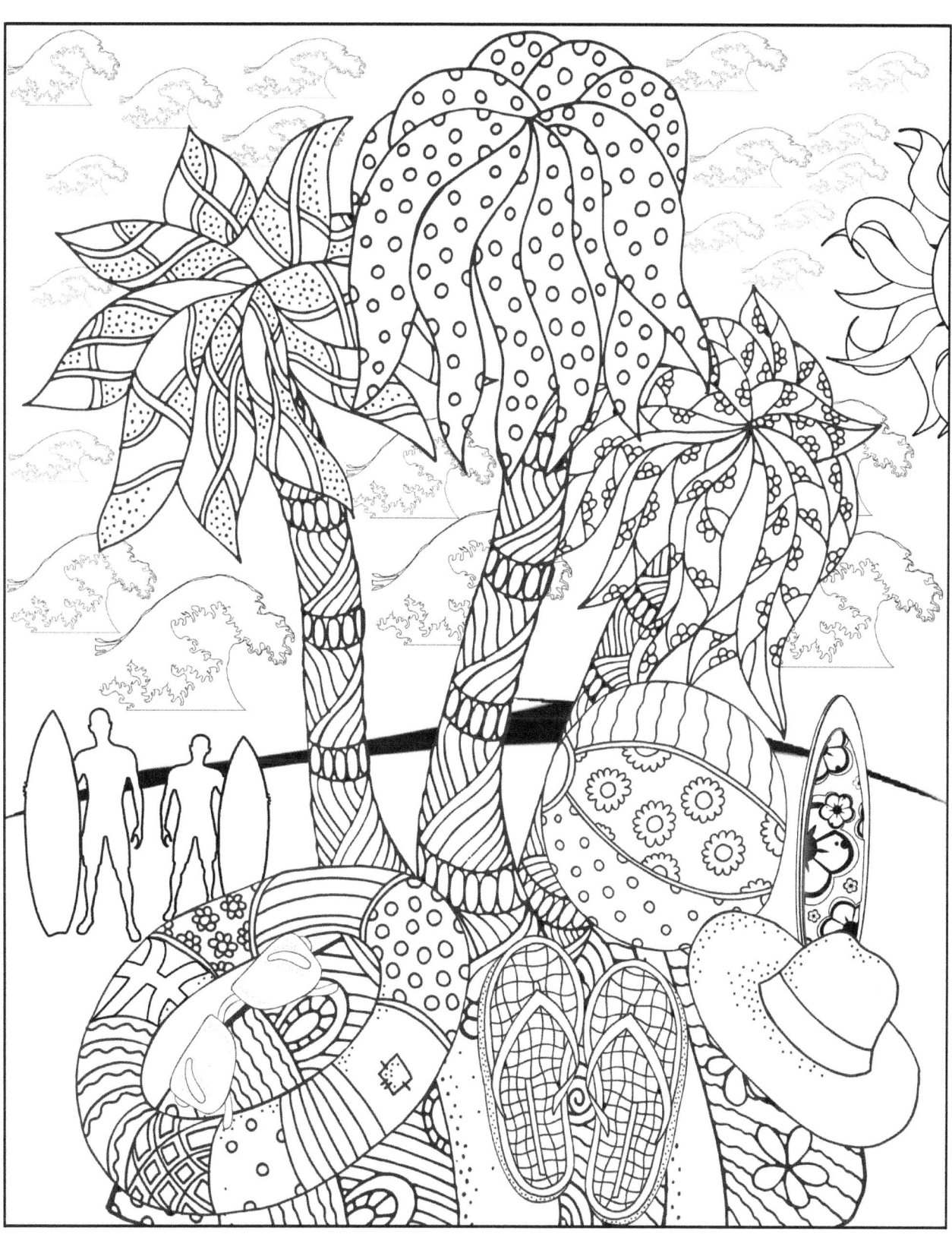

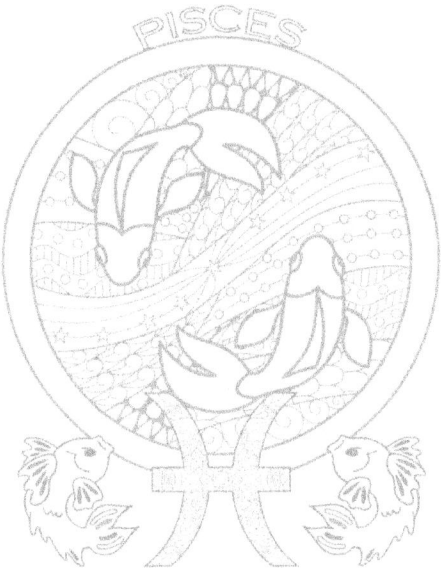

Pisces likes solitude and staying home alone.

_____

_____

_____

_____

_____

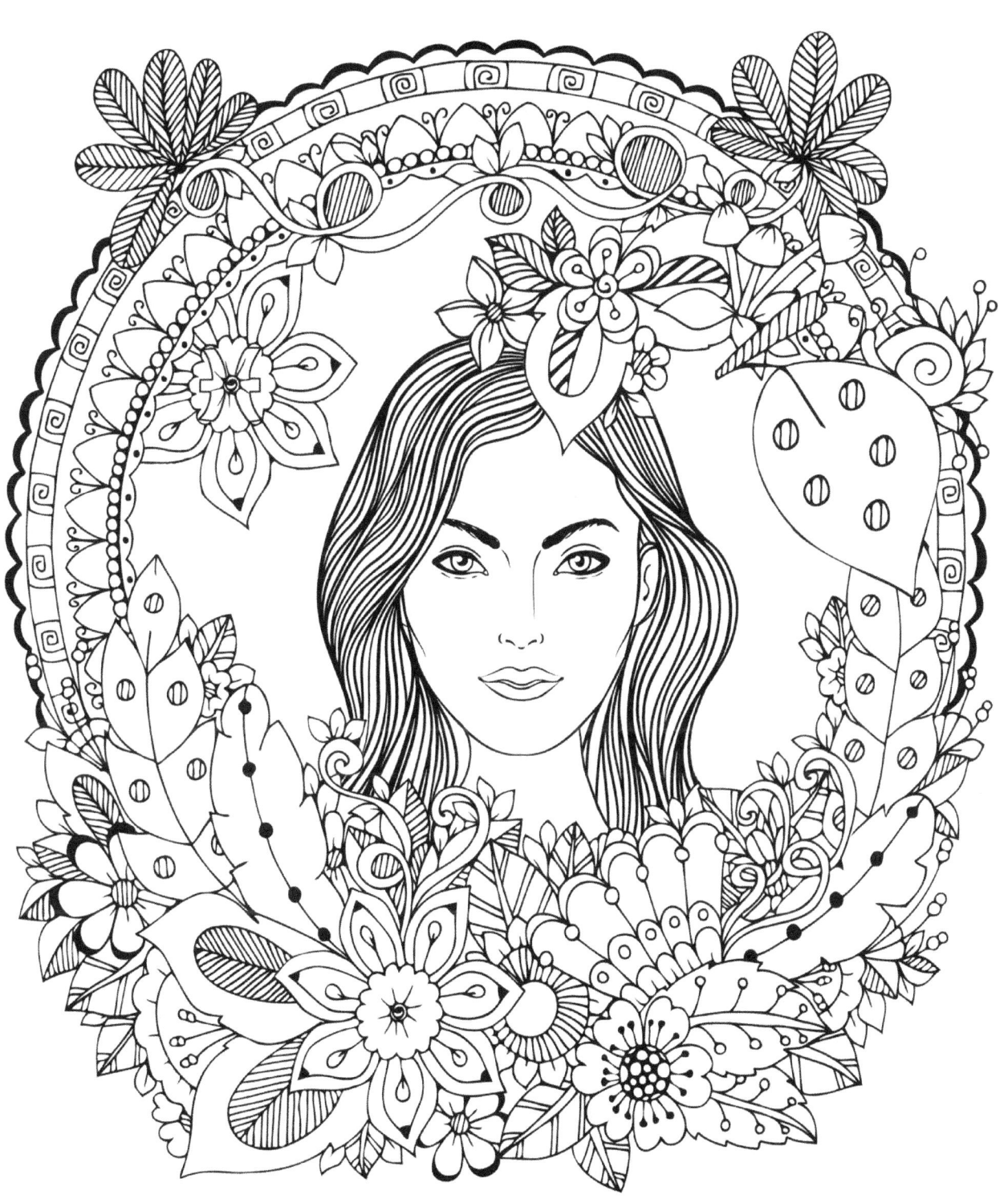

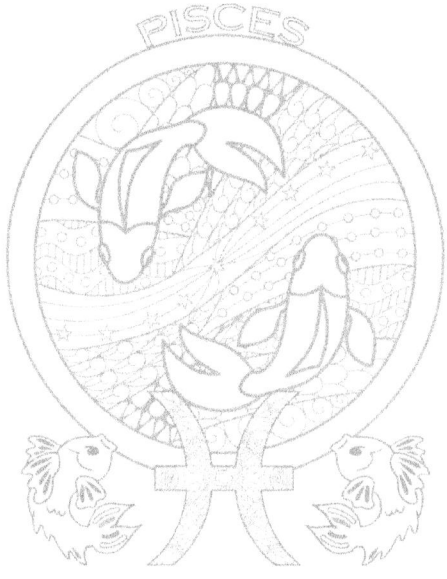

Swimming is often something Pisces loves because of its direct connection to their element of water.

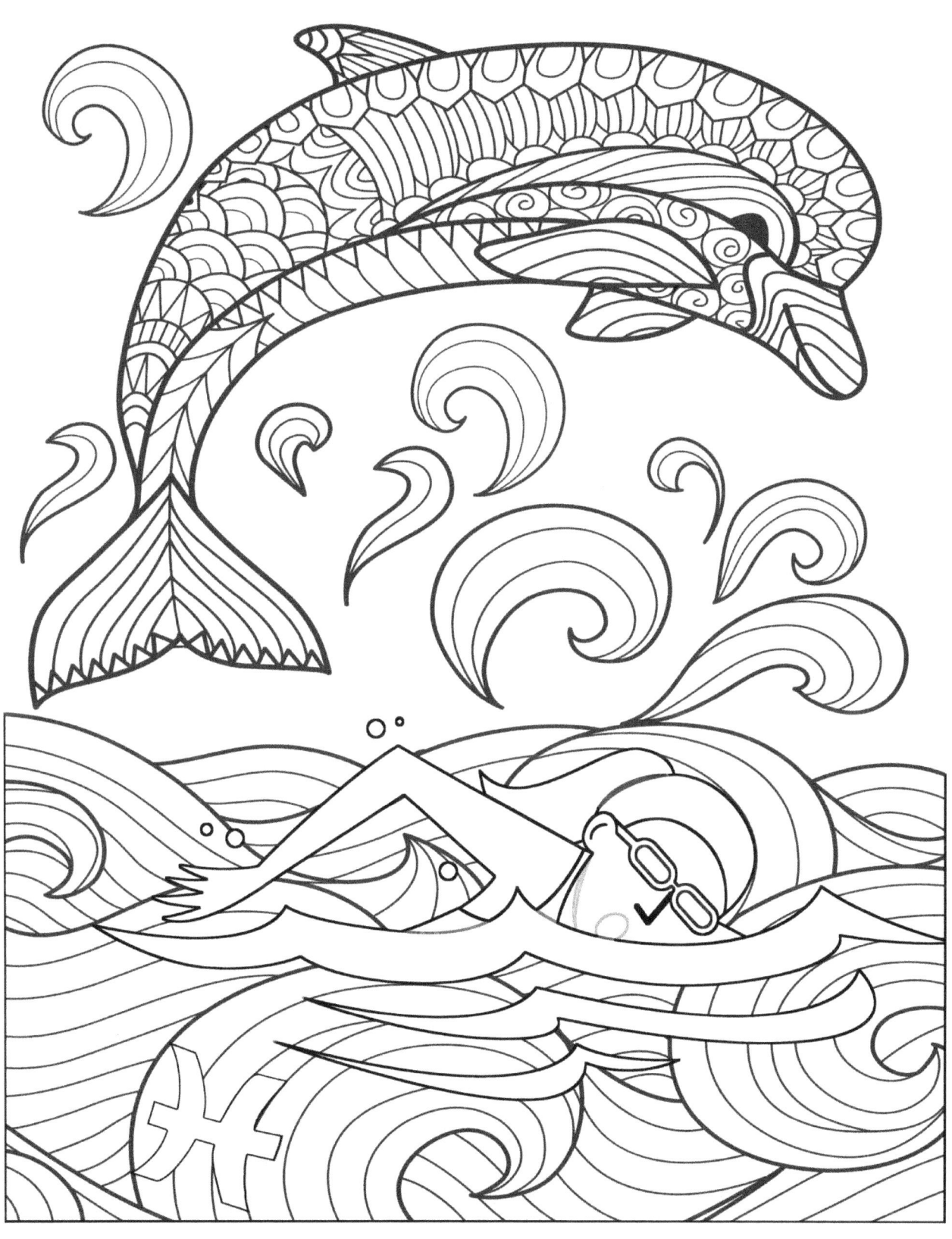

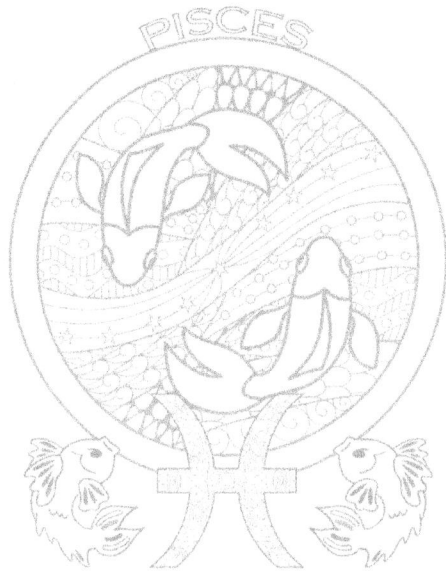

Orchids are considered to be Pisces' flower. They are different, surprising and mysterious.

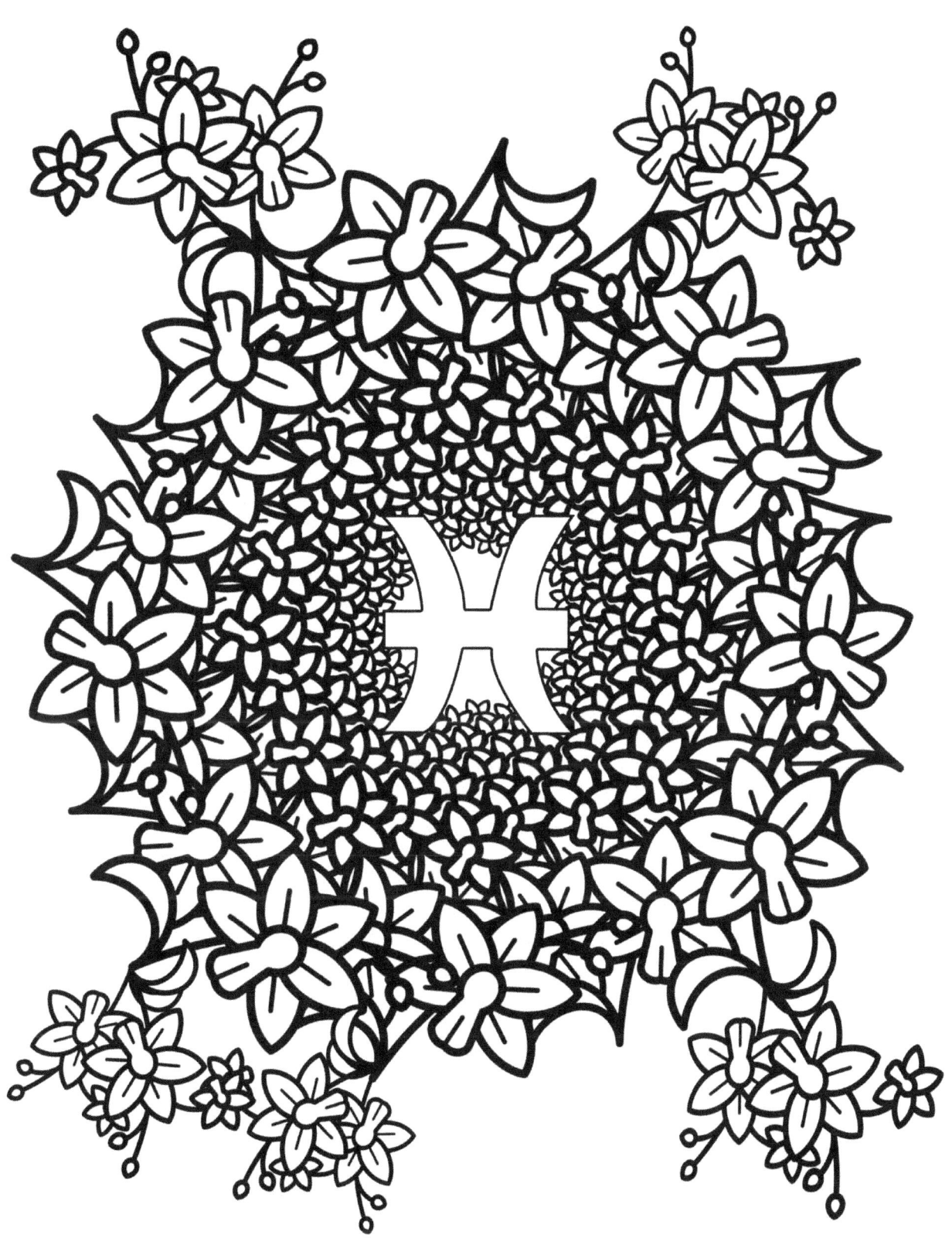

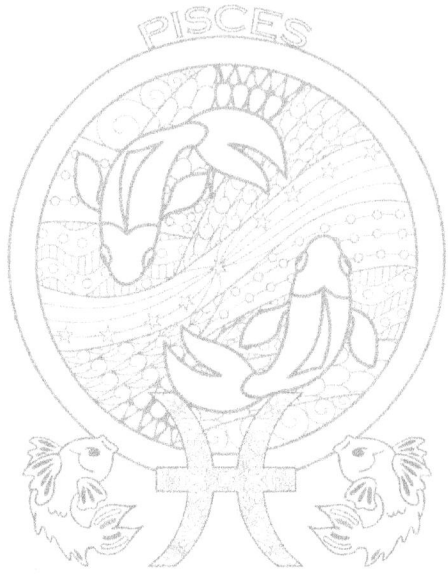

Crystals, dream catchers, essential oils and incense will often find a place in a Pisces' home.

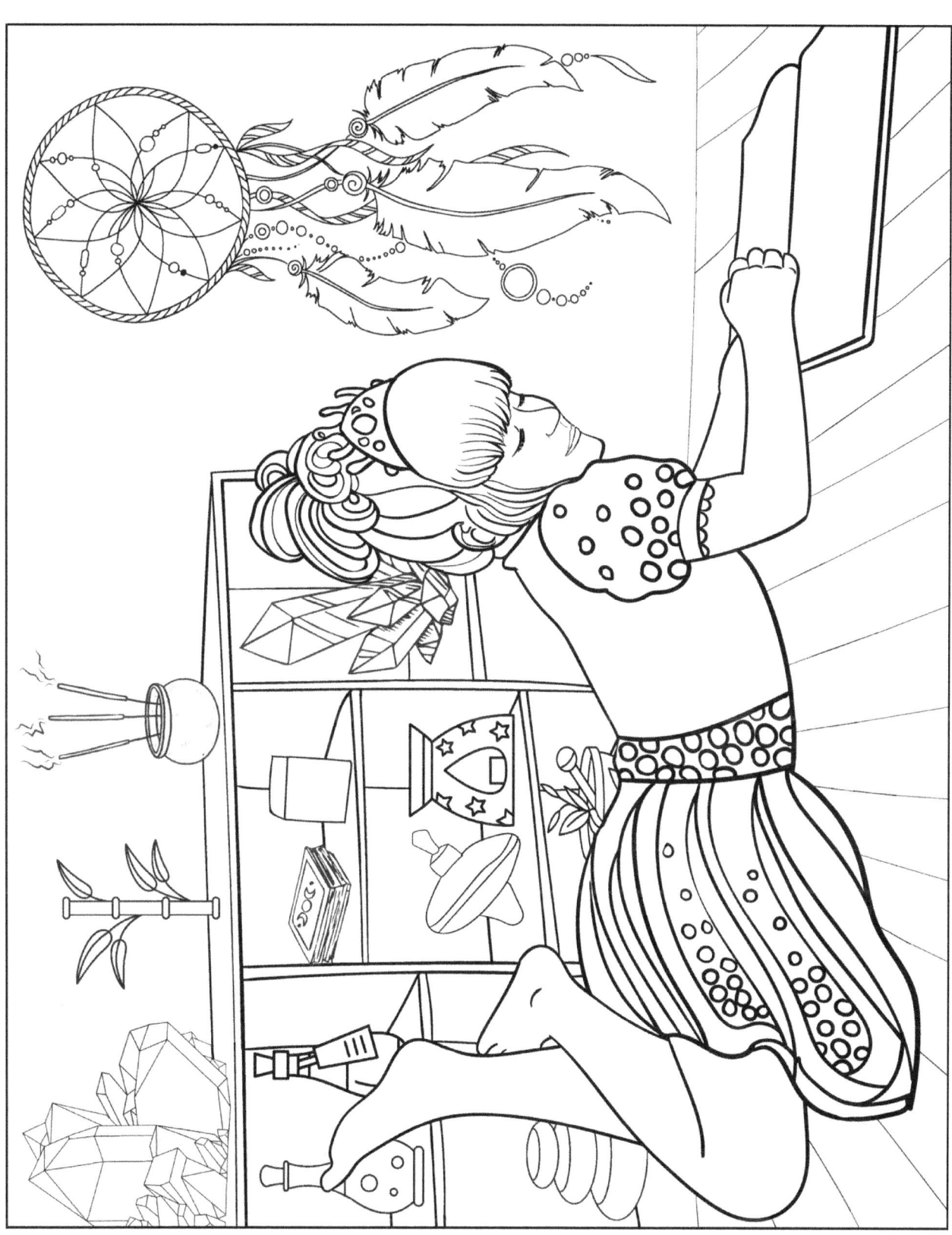

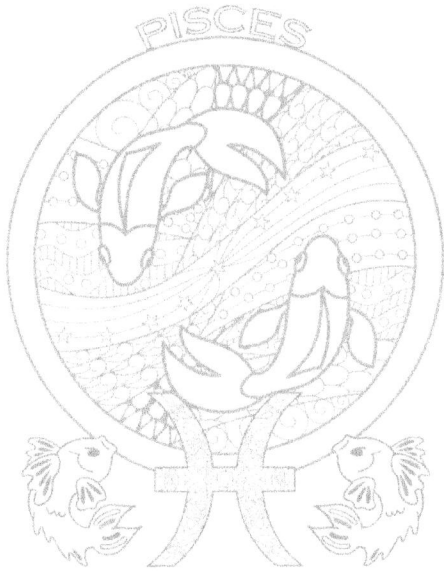

Avid readers, Pisces like books that are dreamy but wise and endlessly creative.

_____

_____

_____

_____

_____

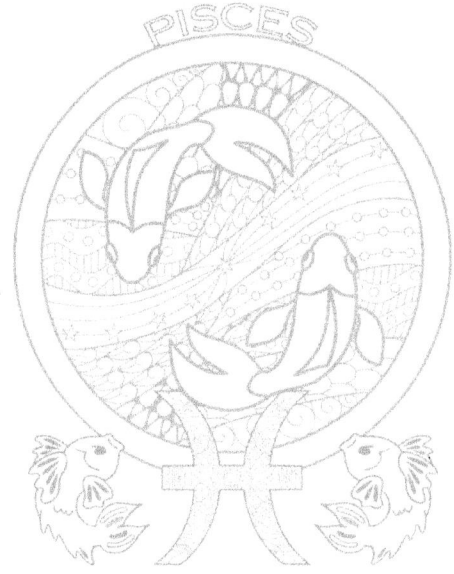

Scuba diving is another activity that puts the watery Pisces in their element.

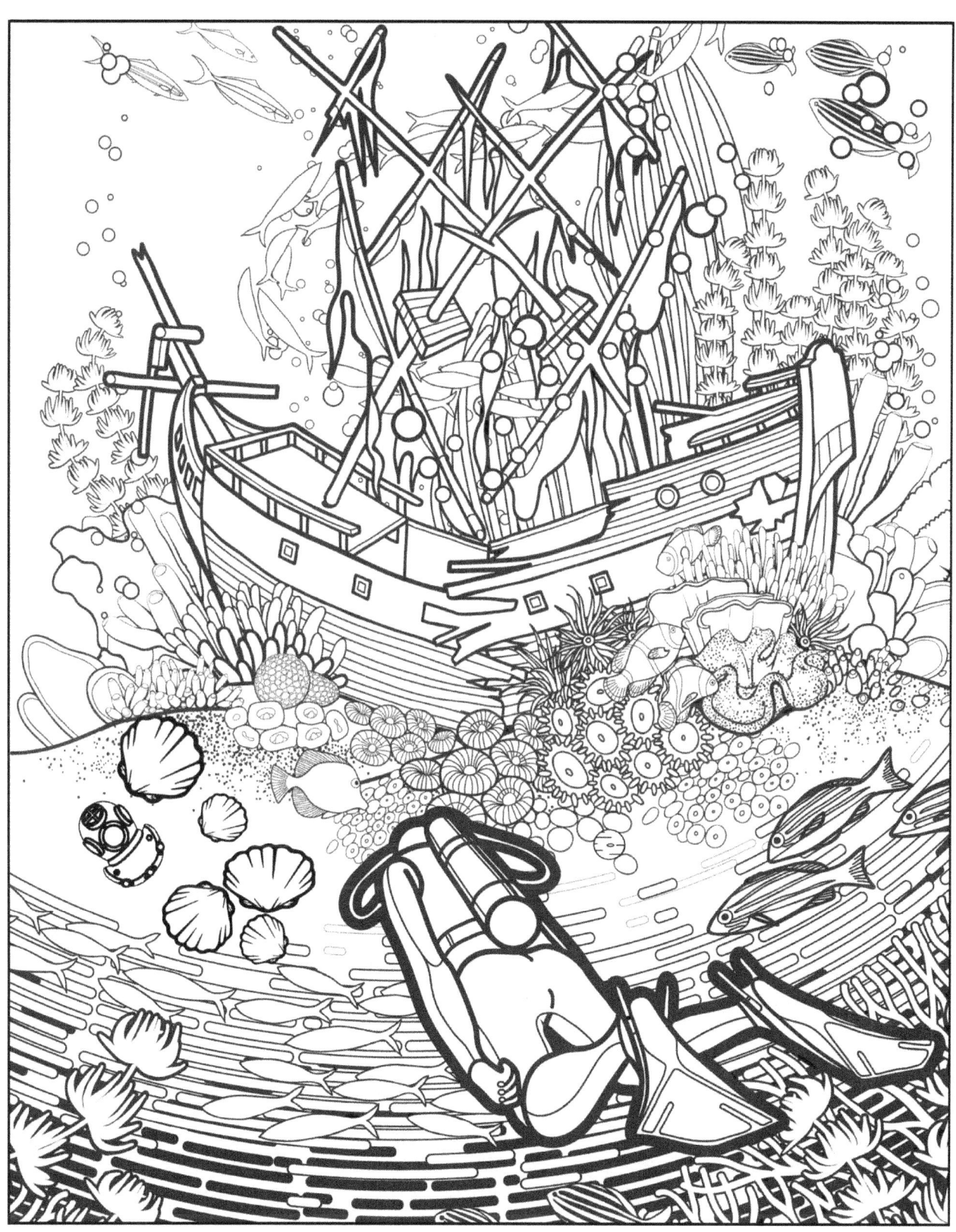

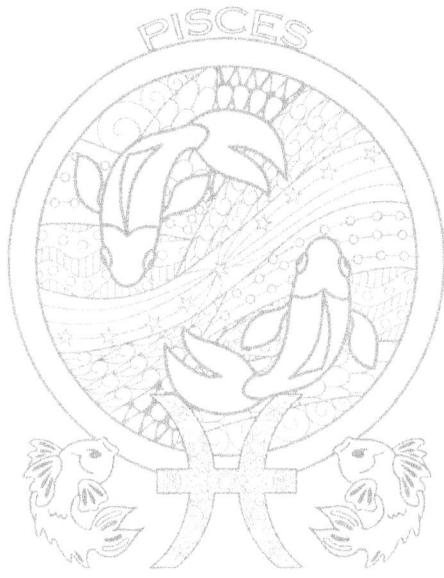

Since Pisces is the sign that rules escapism, fairies often capture their imagination.

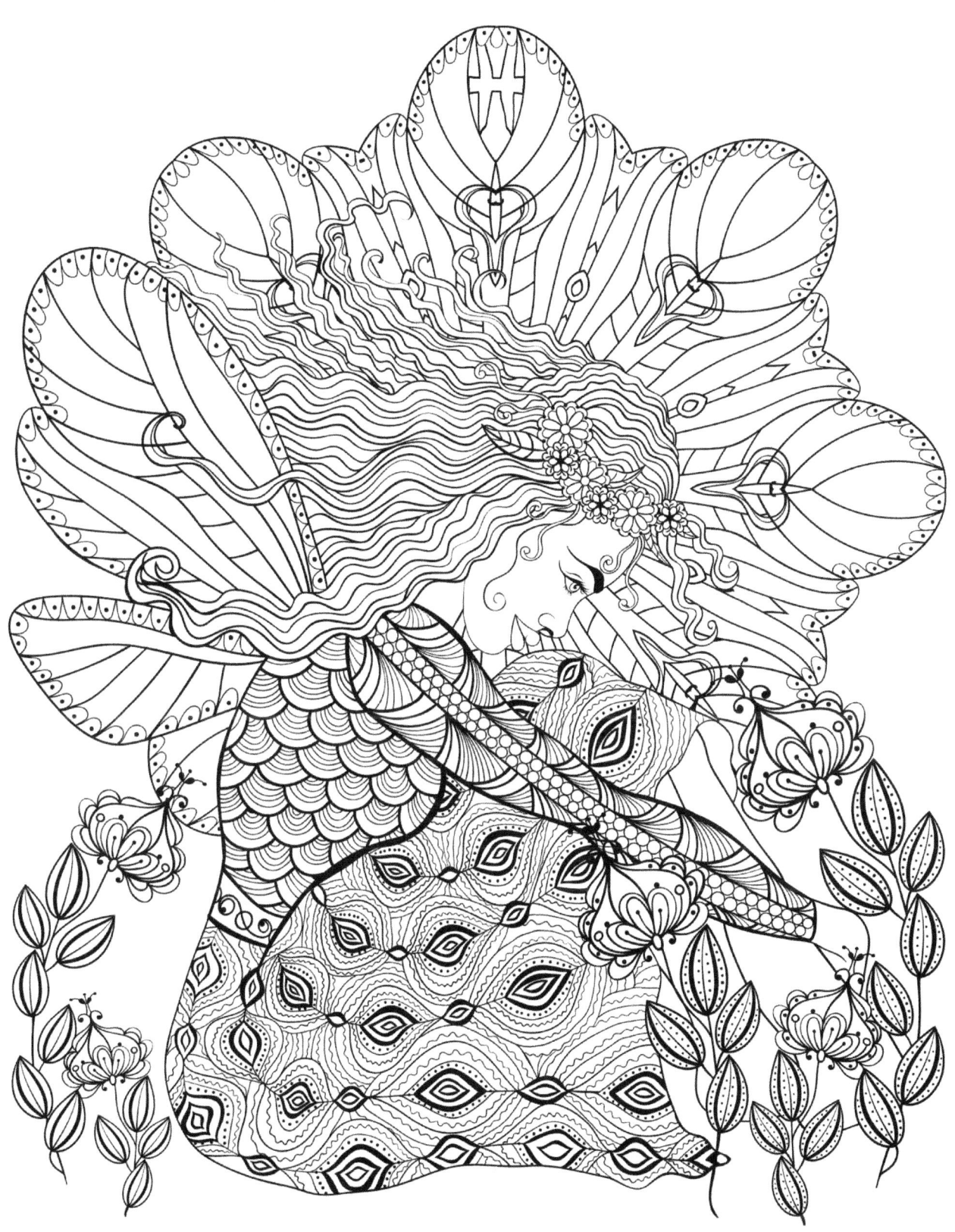

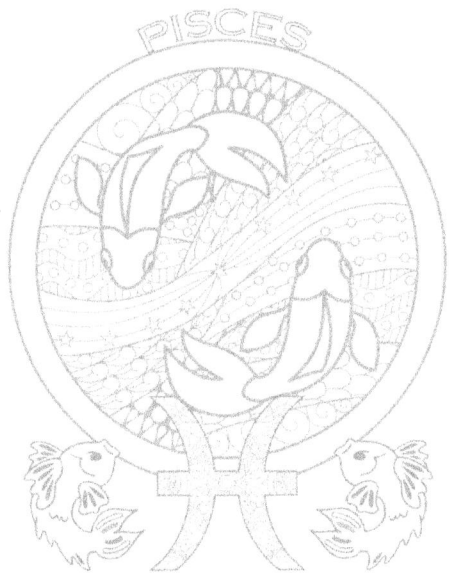

Following a path of solitude toward mystical beauty and truths brought forth from the Pisces' imagination.

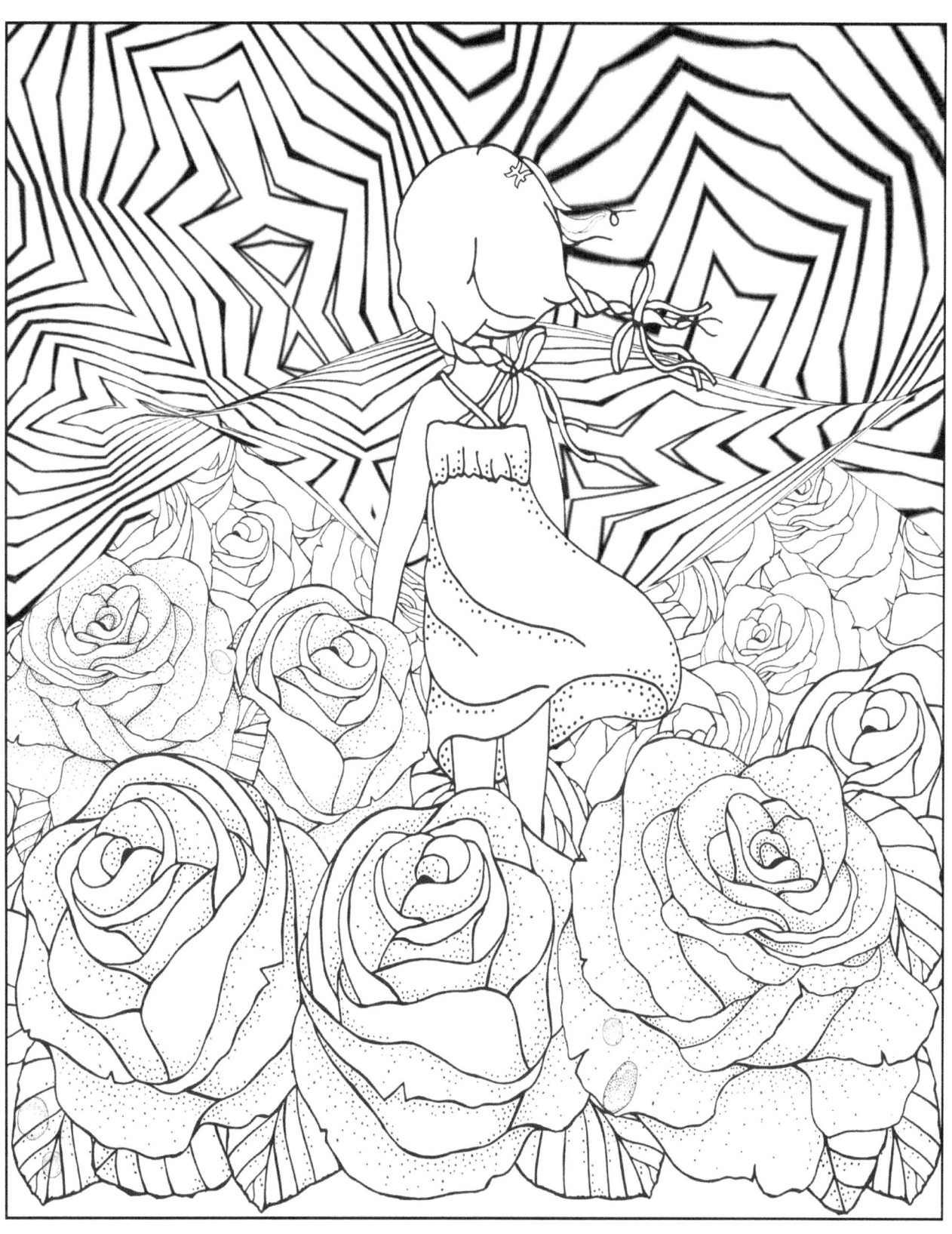

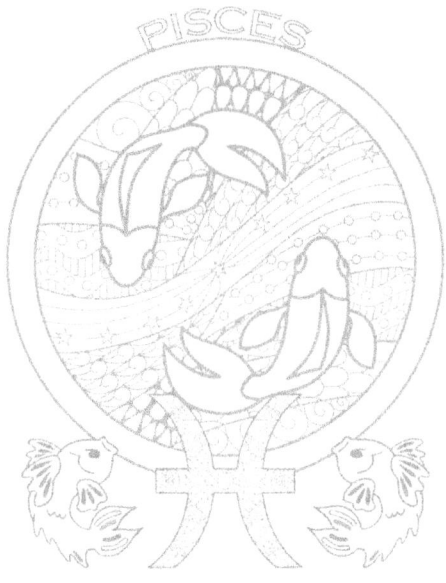

Water lilies are a great plant for Pisces especially in a fish pond.

_____

_____

_____

_____

_____

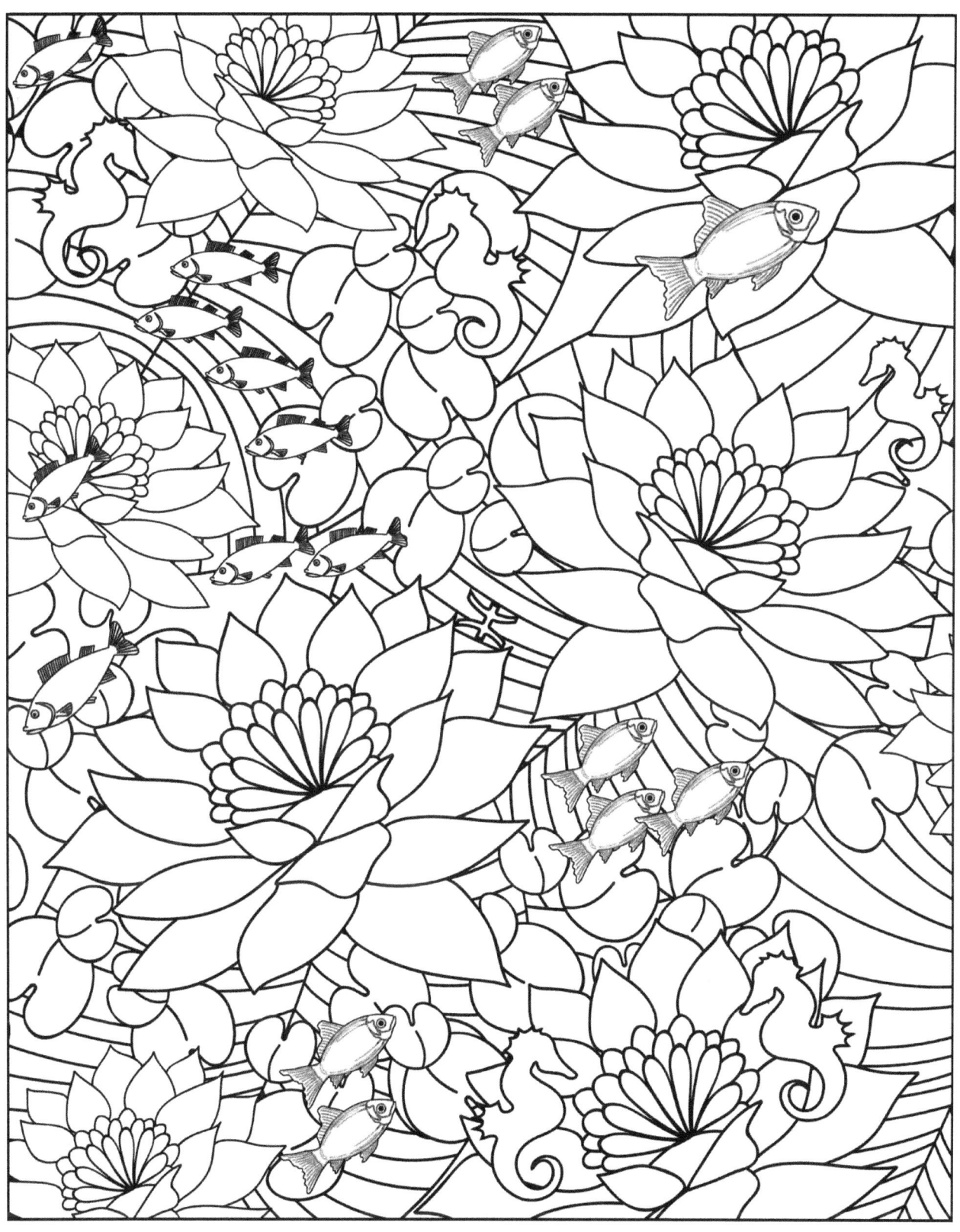

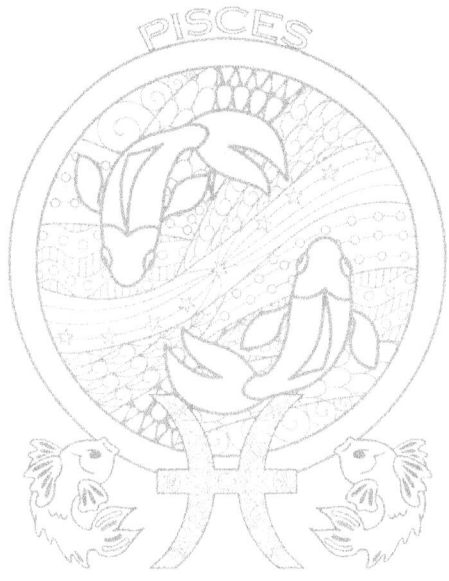

Touching hands reflect the compassion and understanding possessed by so many Pisceans.

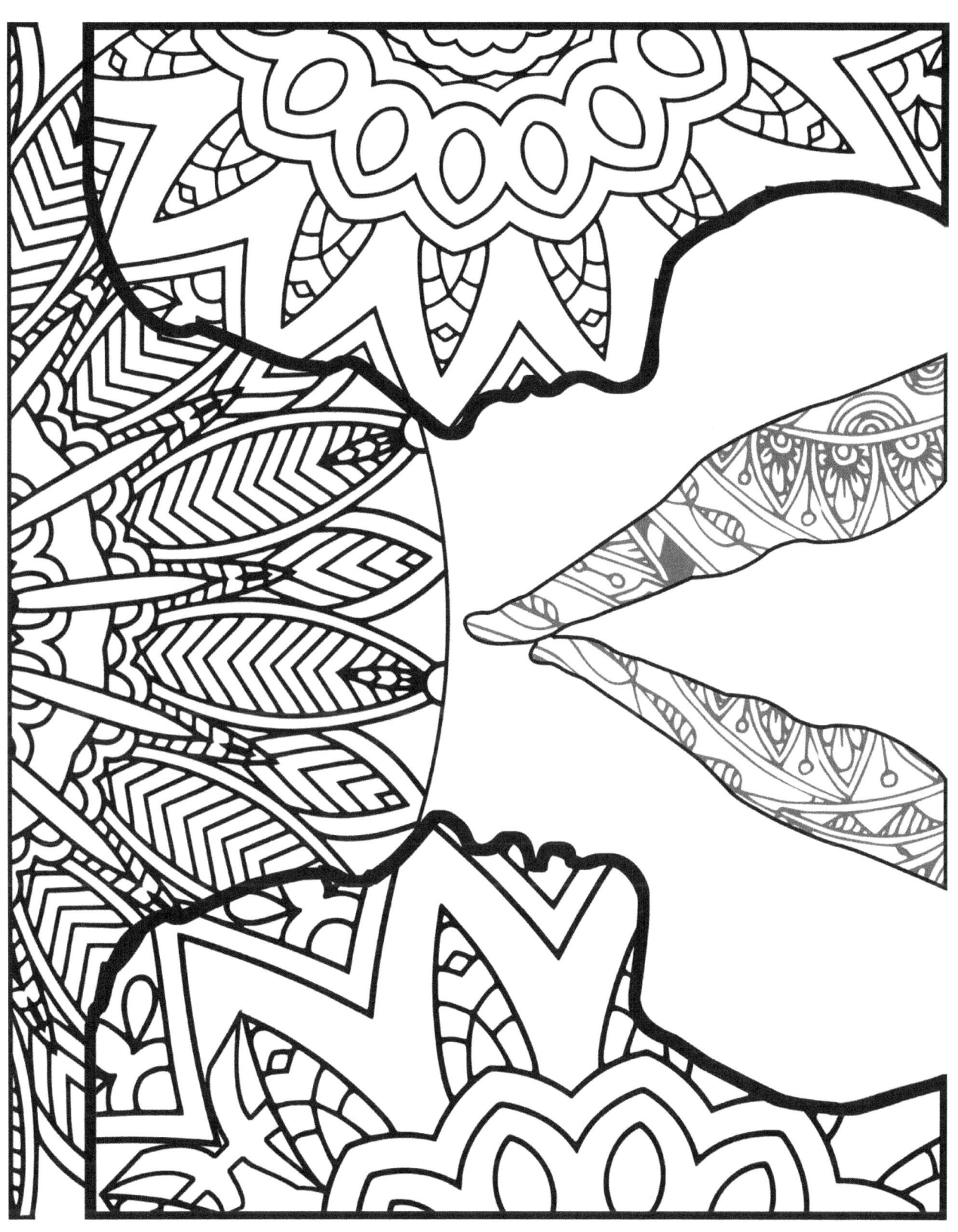

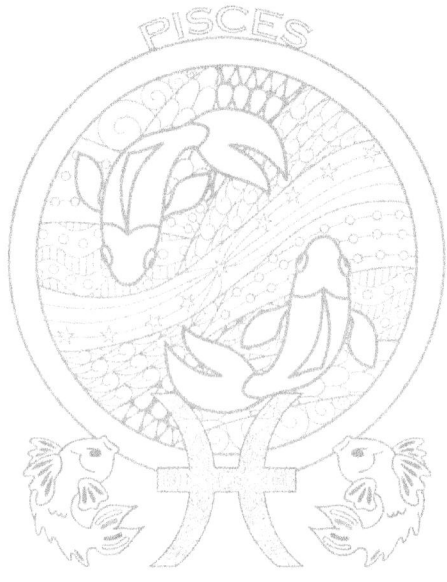

A watery dream with ships, fish and the ocean suits the Pisces wonderfully.

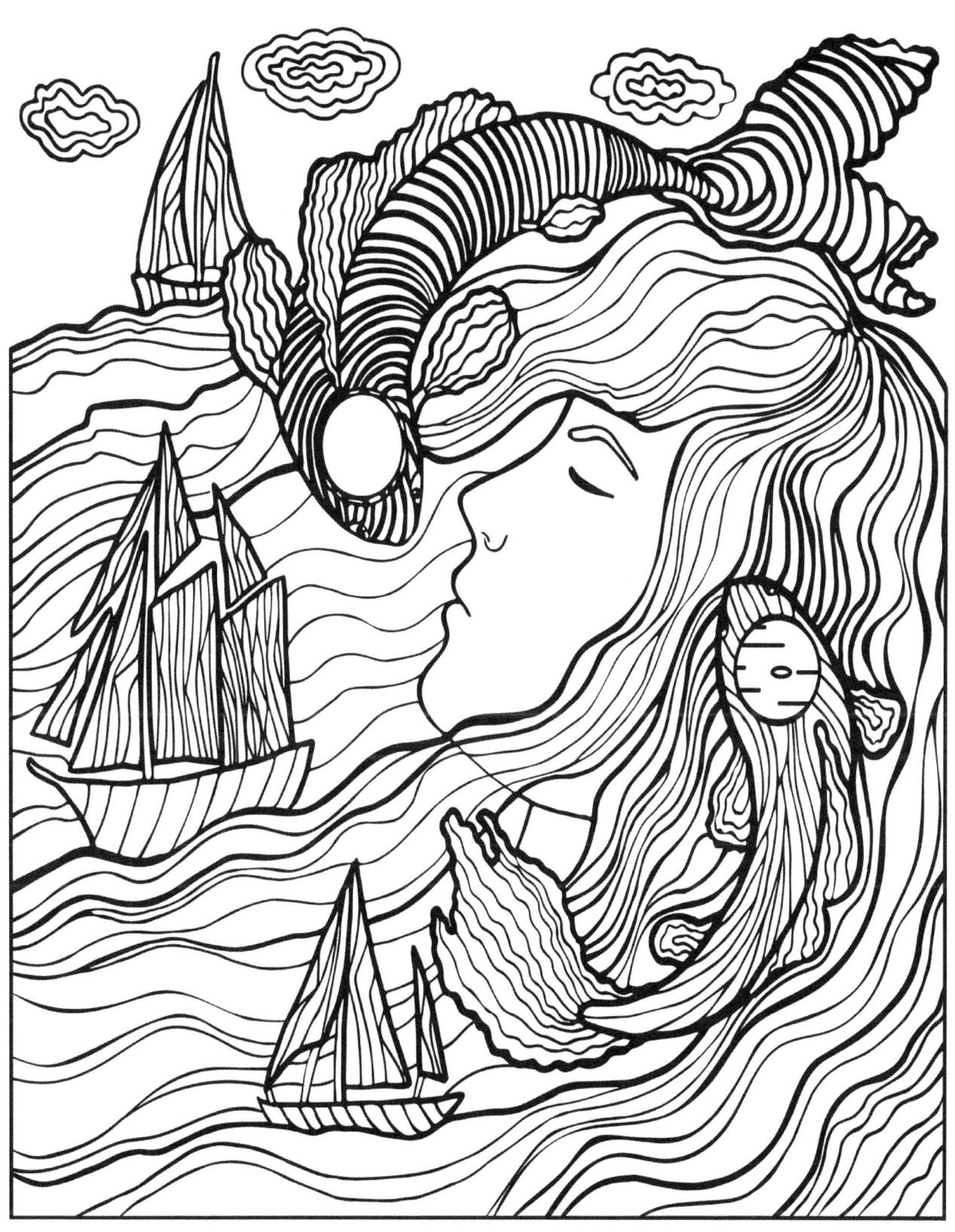

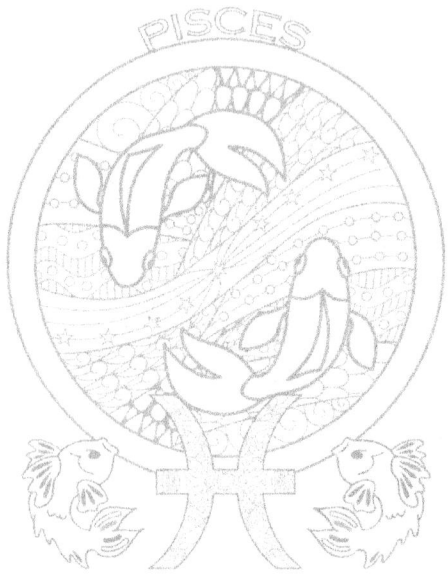

Combining Pisces' flower, the orchid, with the mystical and mysterious creates an artistic burst.

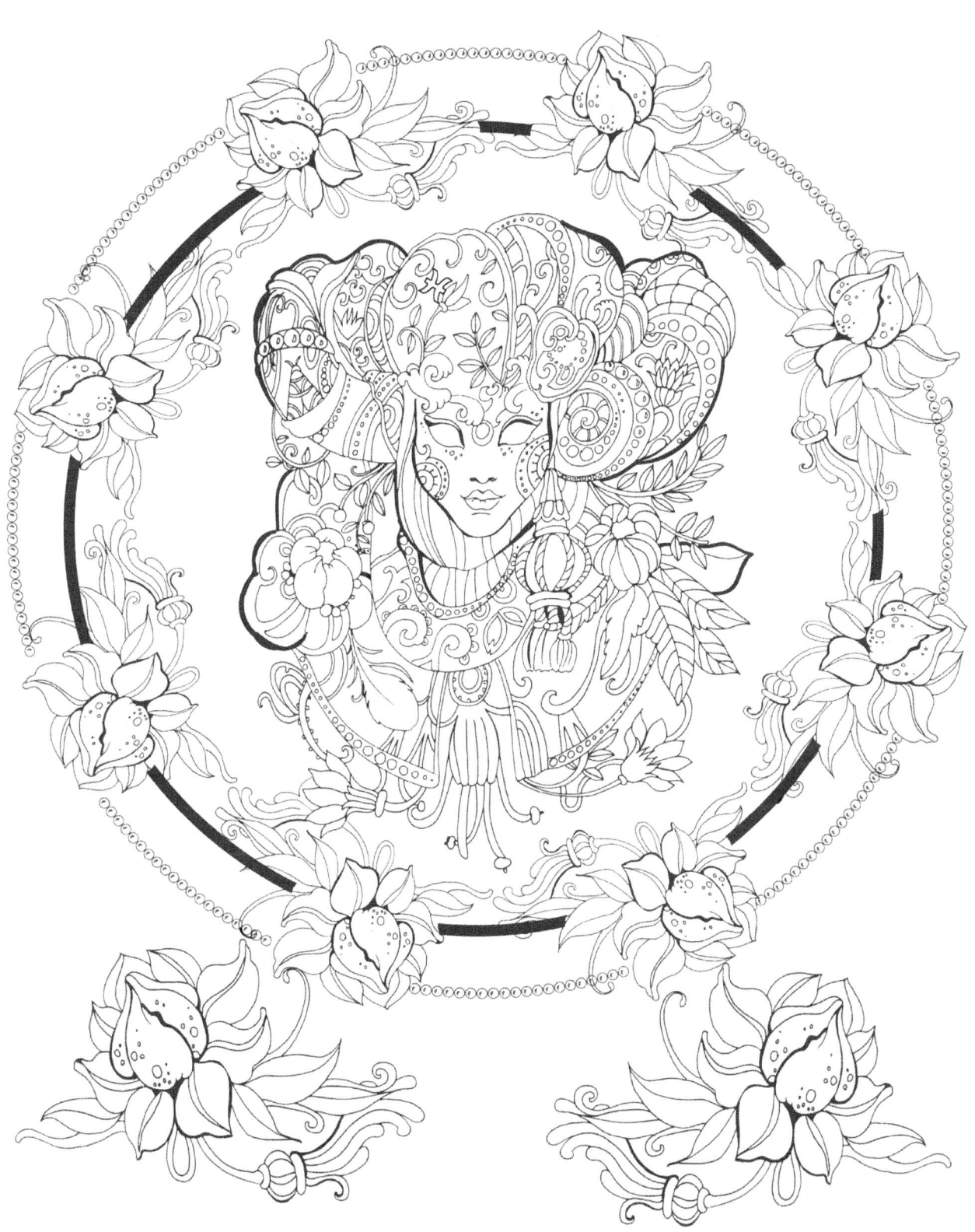

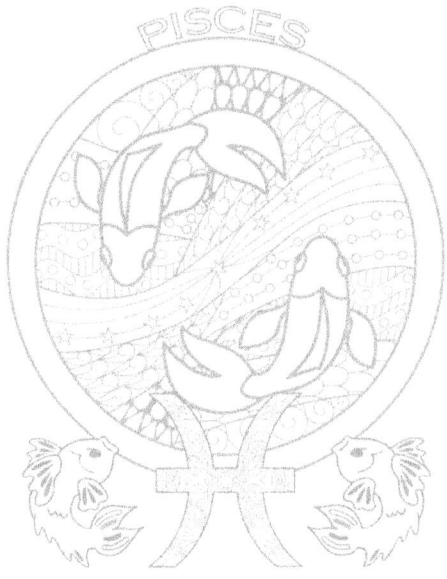

Pisceans are very in tune with unseen and mystical forces, and are far more likely to have psychic abilities.

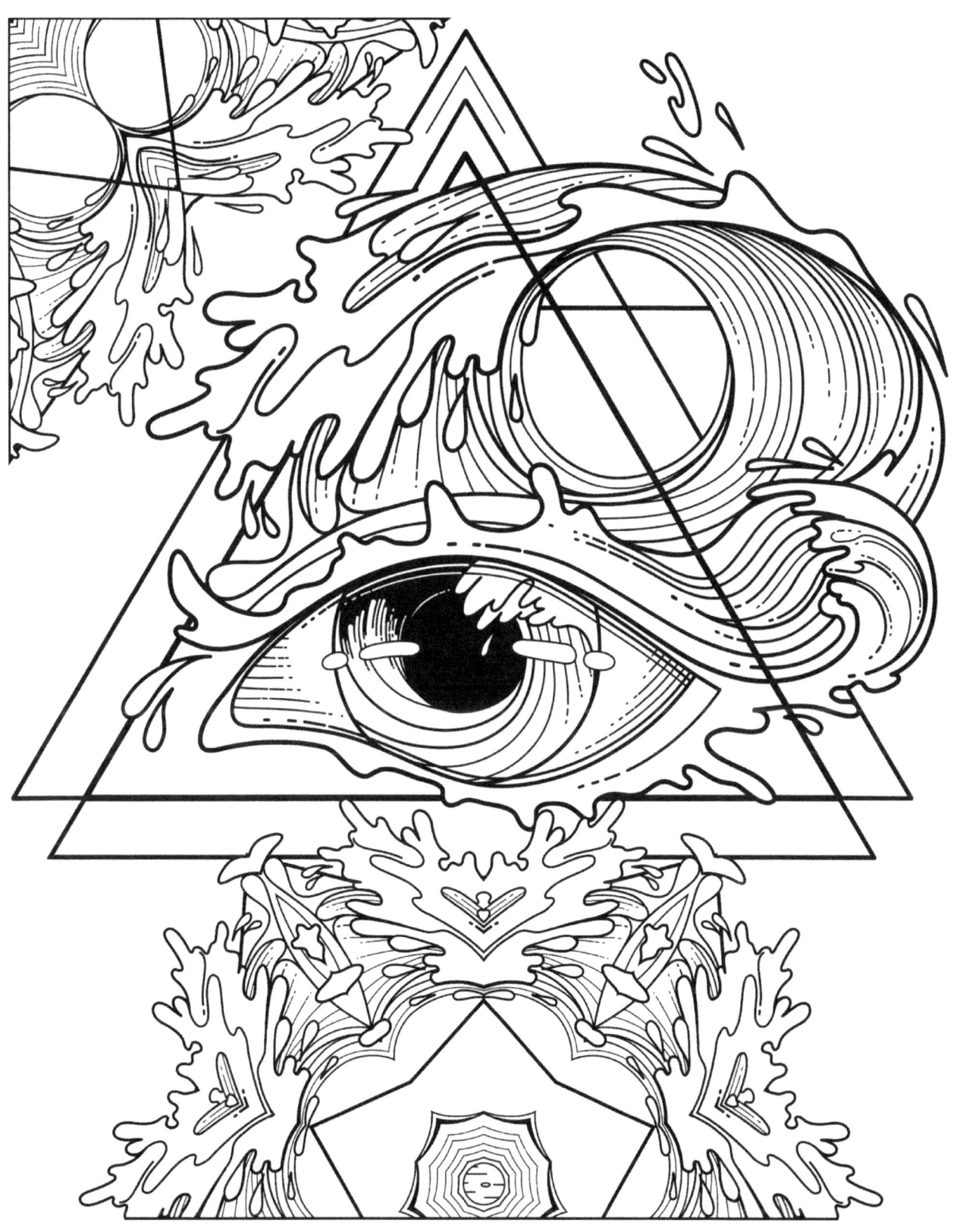

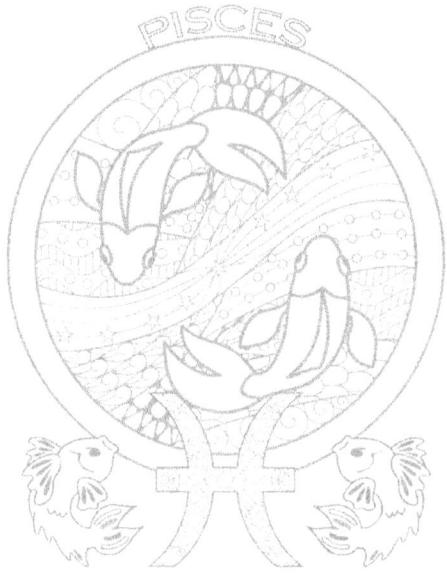

Pisces Mandala - Neptune, Water, Alder Leaves, Fish, Orchids

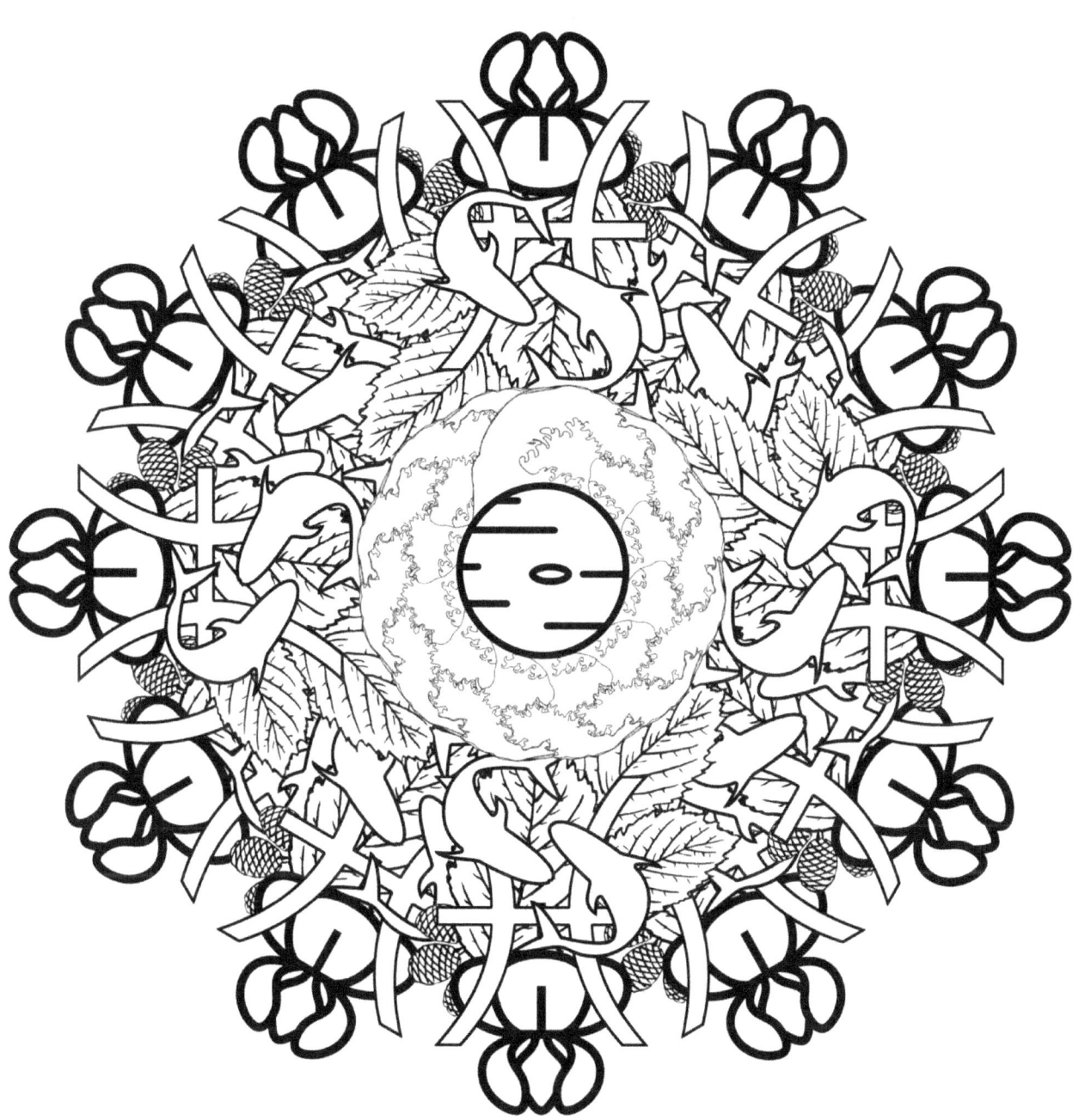

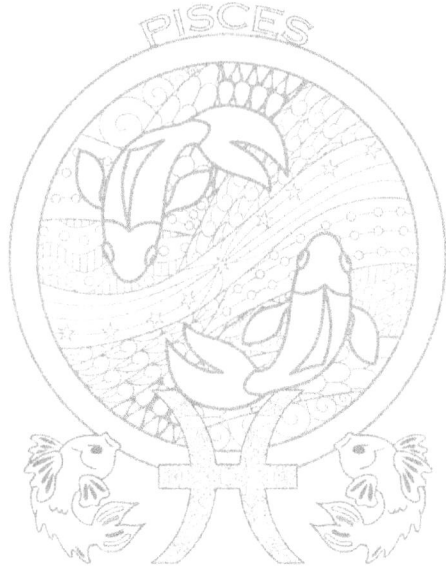

Dreaming can be an escape but also a connection for the wise souls of Pisces.

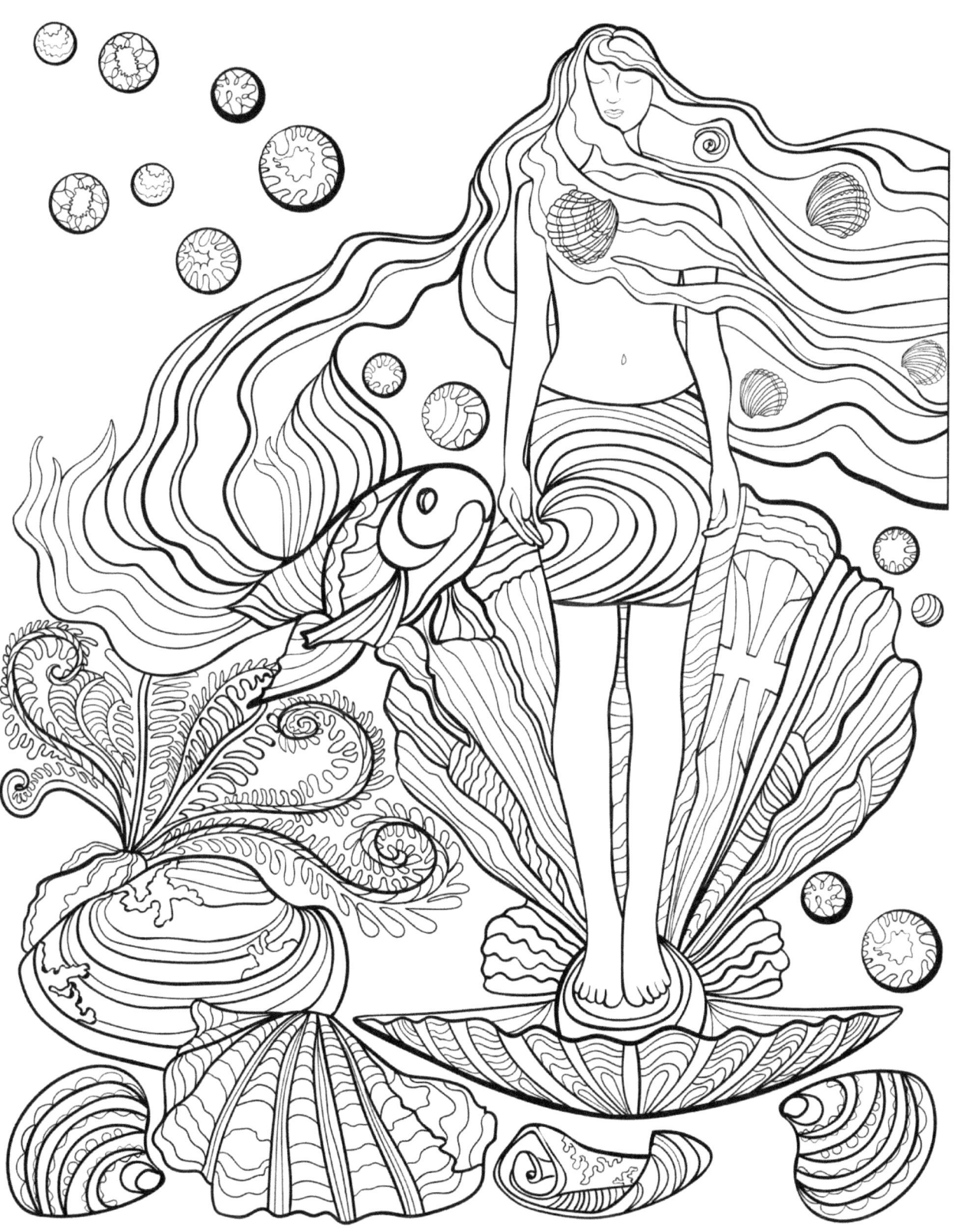

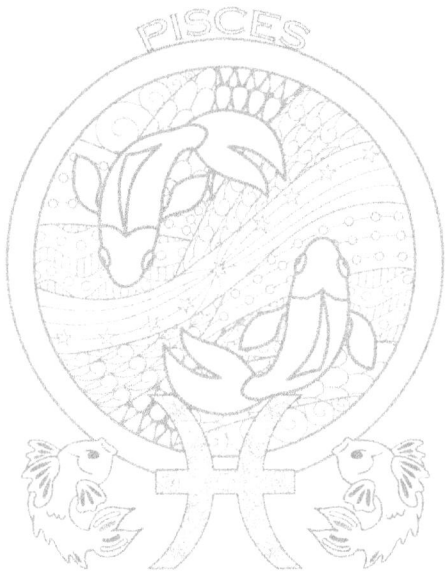

Being ruled by Neptune, planet of illusions, makes Pisces excellent at acting but can sometimes lead to self-deception.

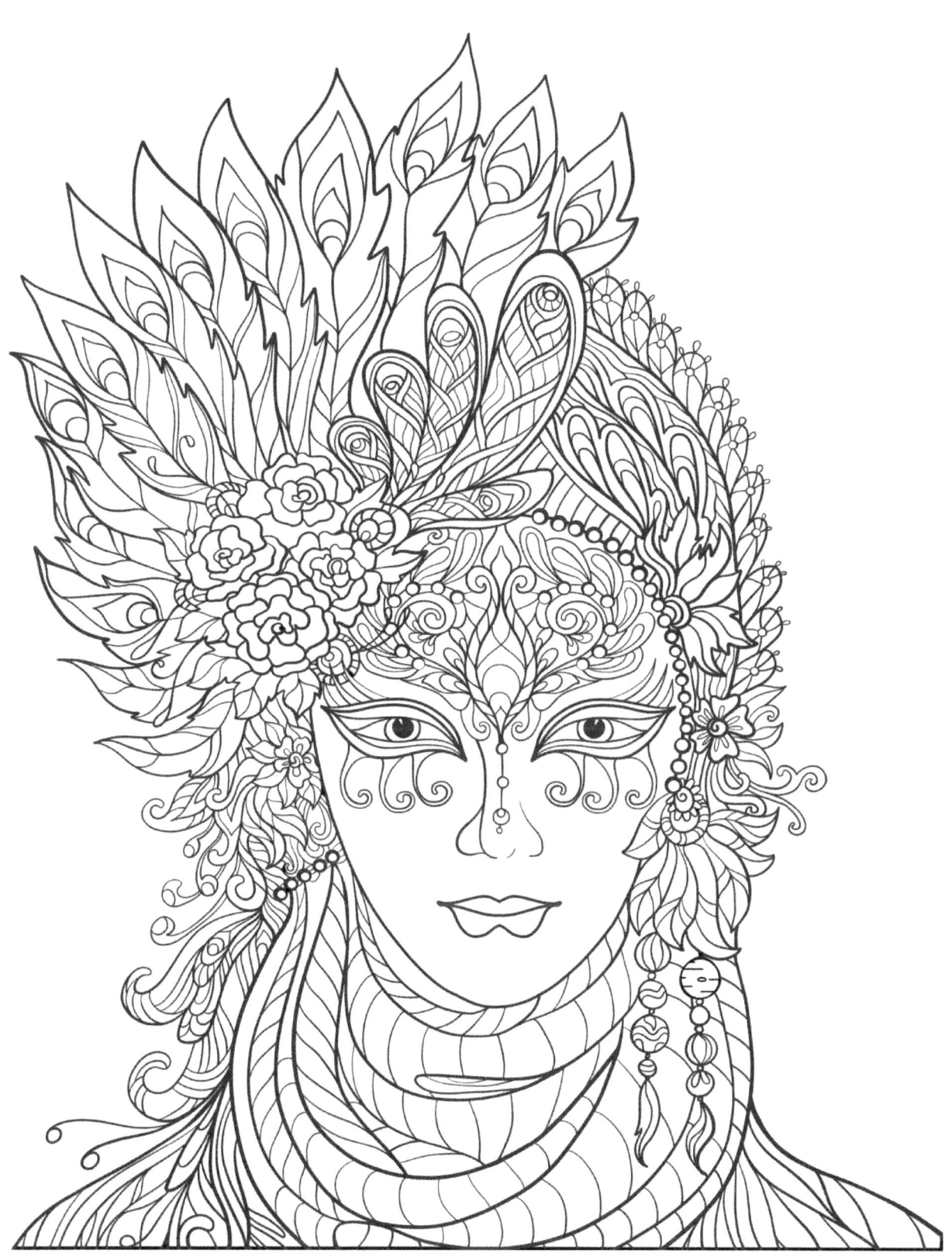

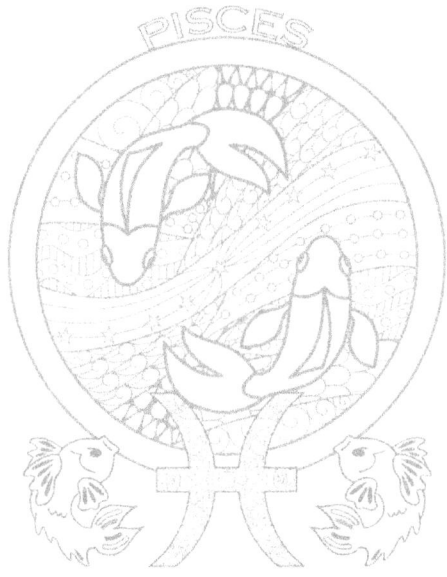

Even if they aren't musicians, Pisces love music and often use it as a communication tool.

_____

_____

_____

_____

_____

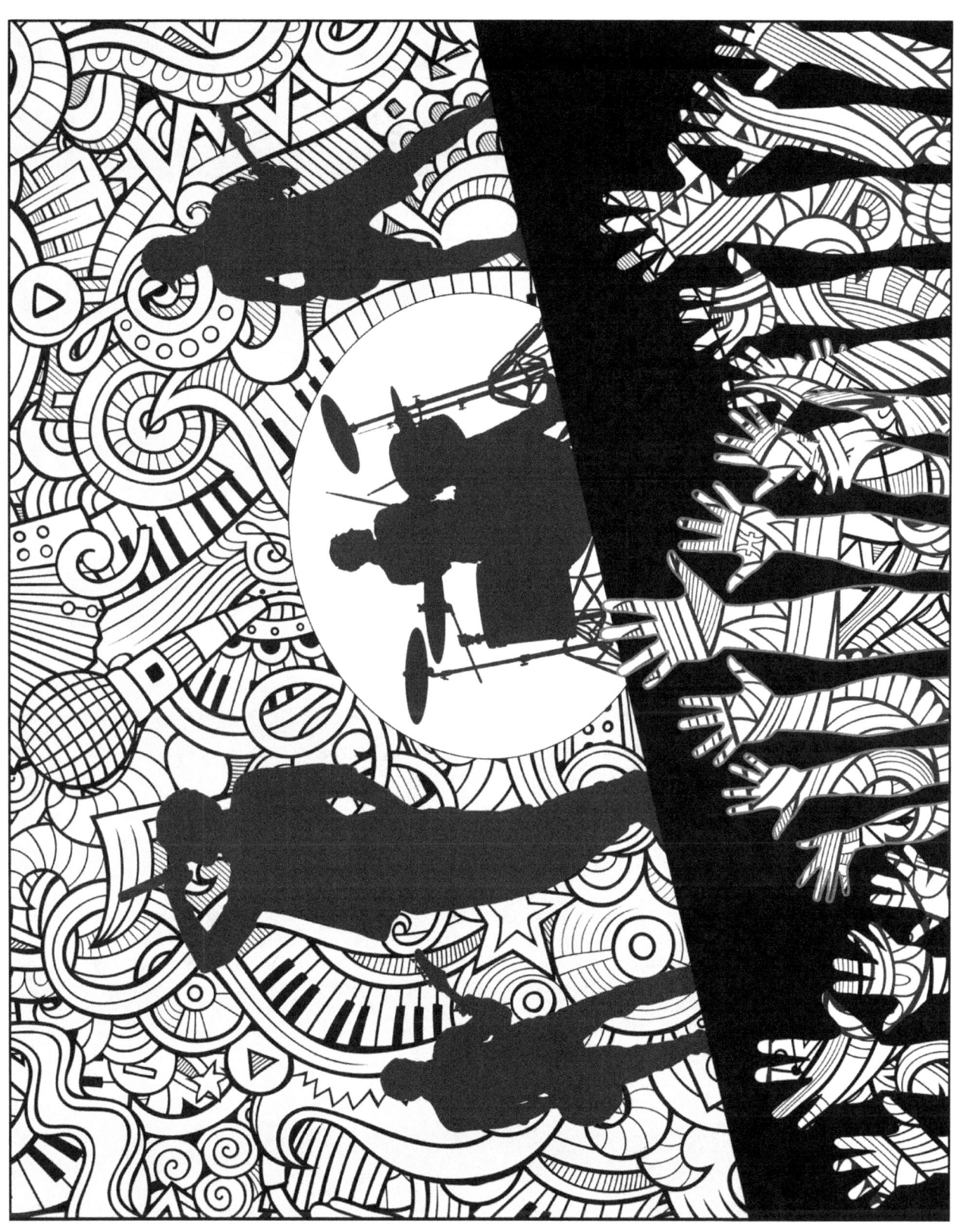

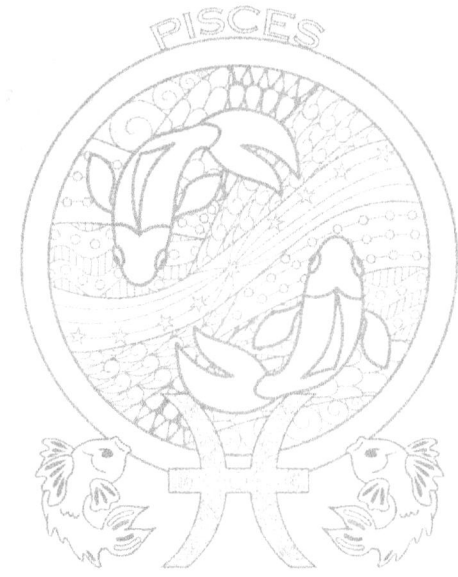

Sea shells are a wonderful way to keep the Pisces connected to the ocean.

_____

_____

_____

_____

_____

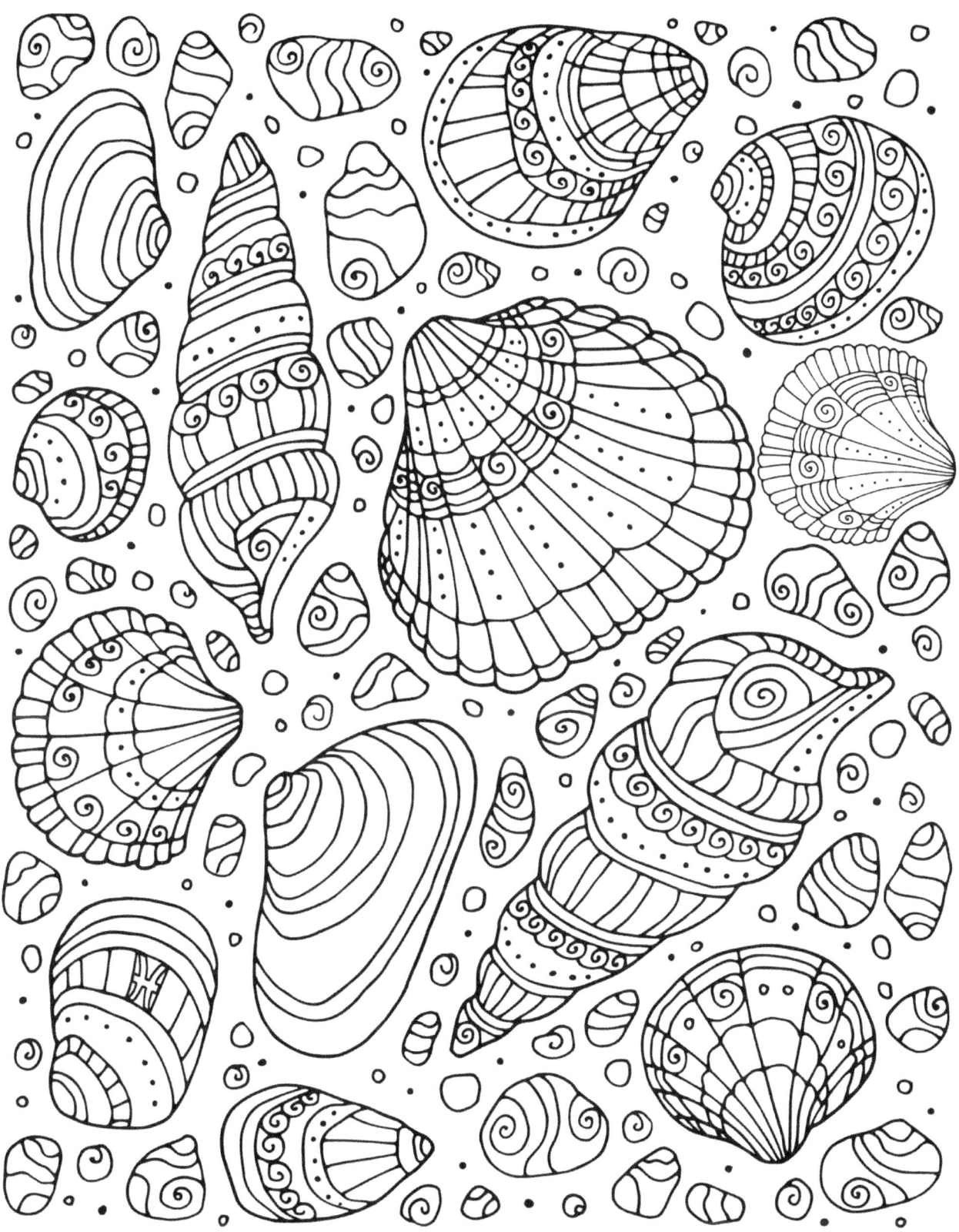

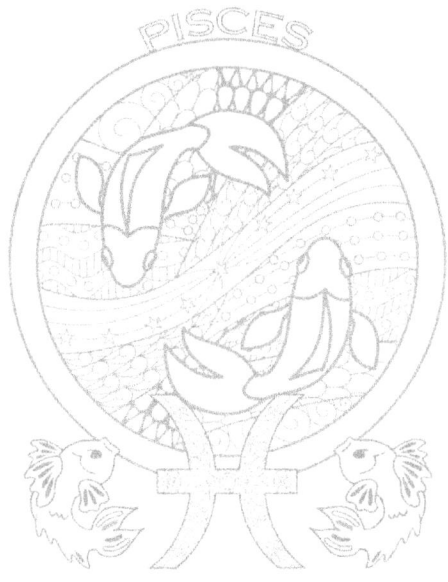

Pisceans like to spend time away from the everyday material world and in the realm of spirit and mind.

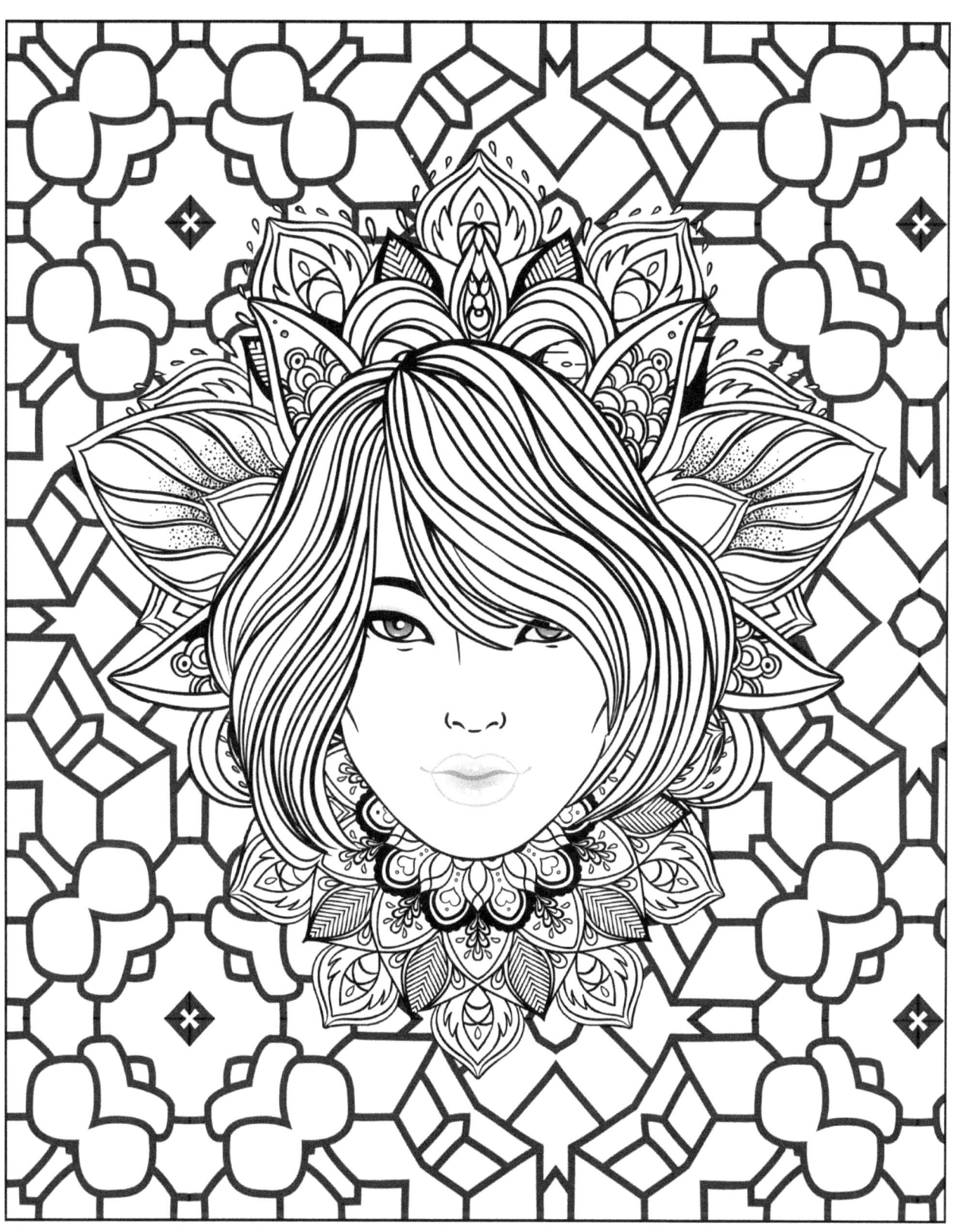

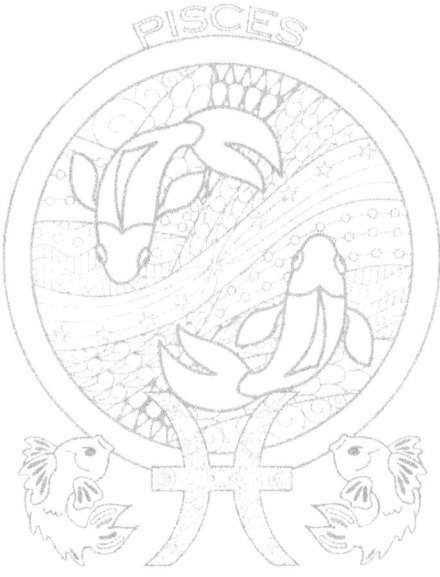

Highly emotional souls, Pisces can often be quite romantic.

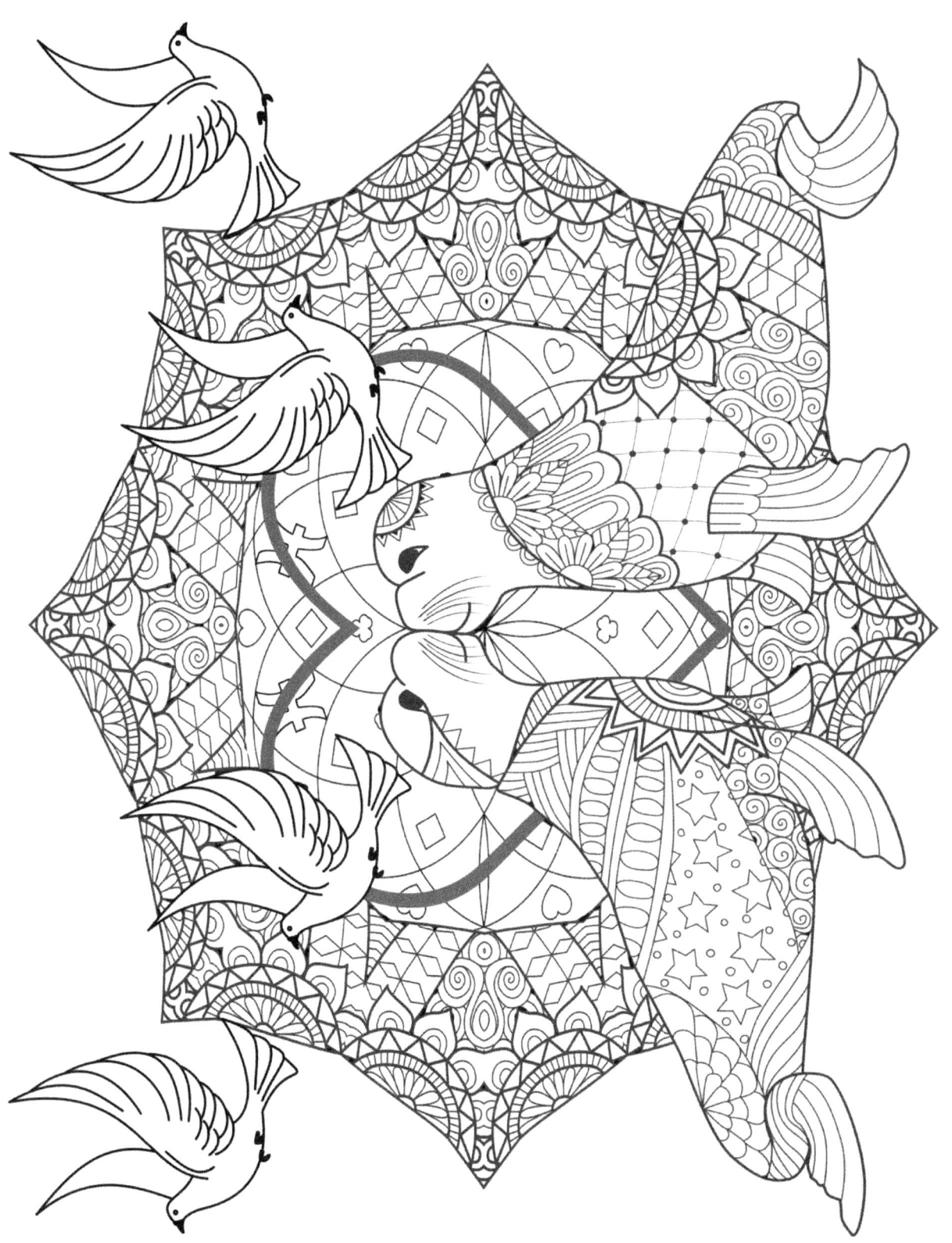

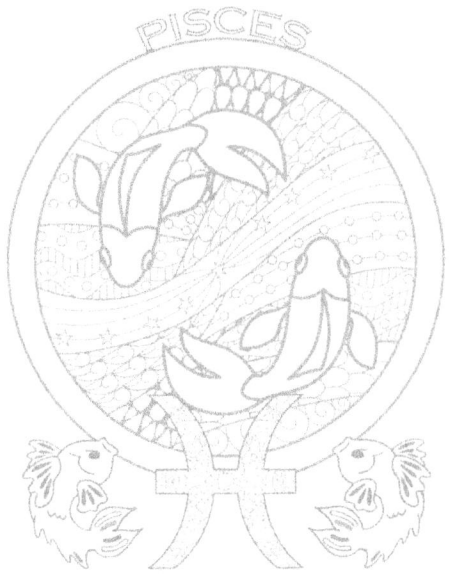

Dear Pisces - close your eyes and dream, connect, feel.

_____

_____

_____

_____

_____

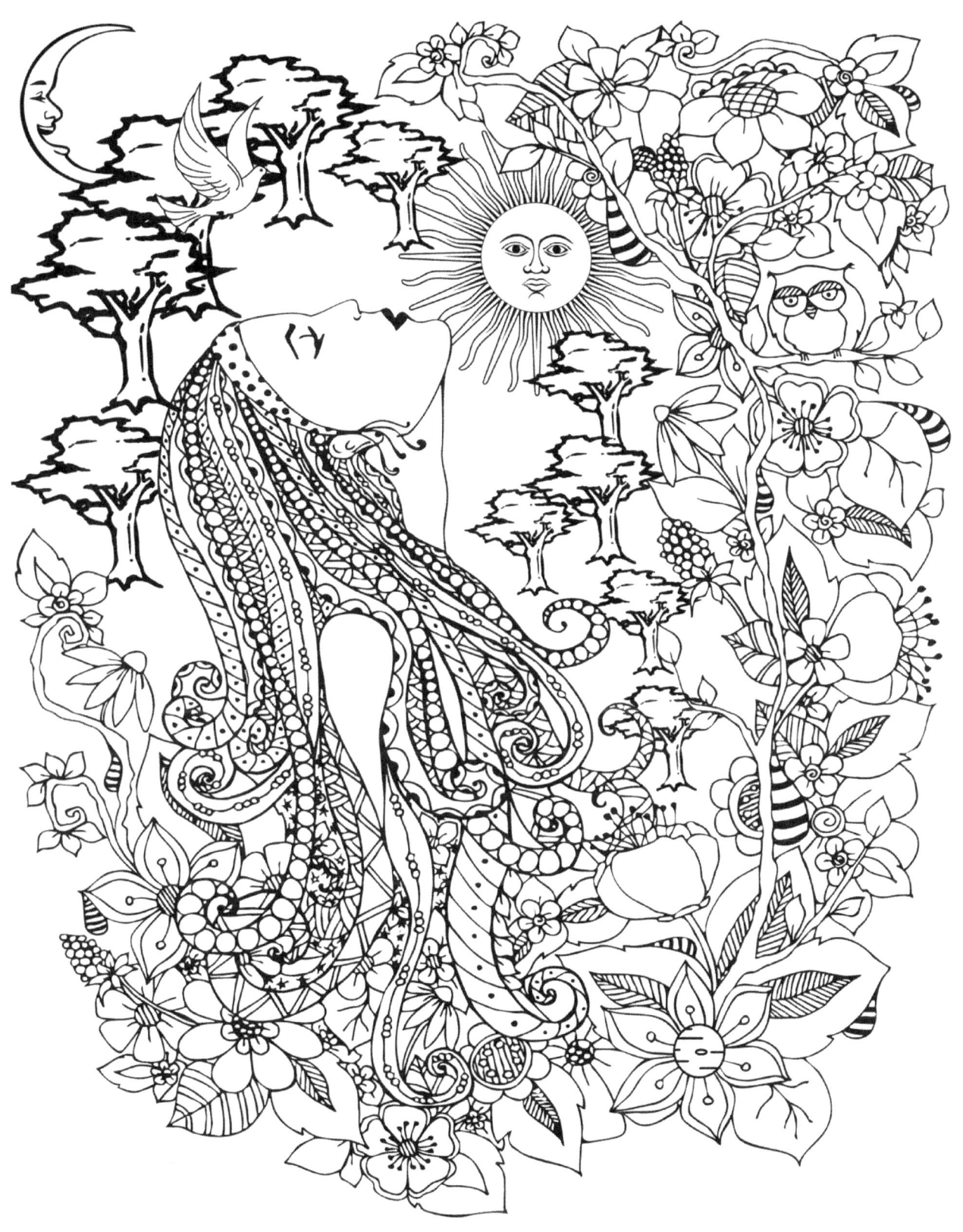

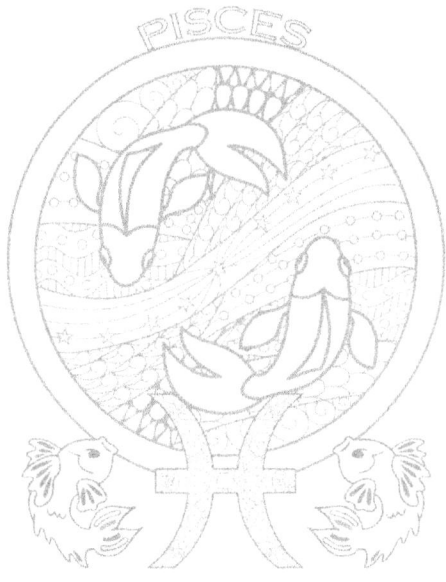

Since Pisces rules the feet and dancing is another creative expression, many Pisceans love to dance.

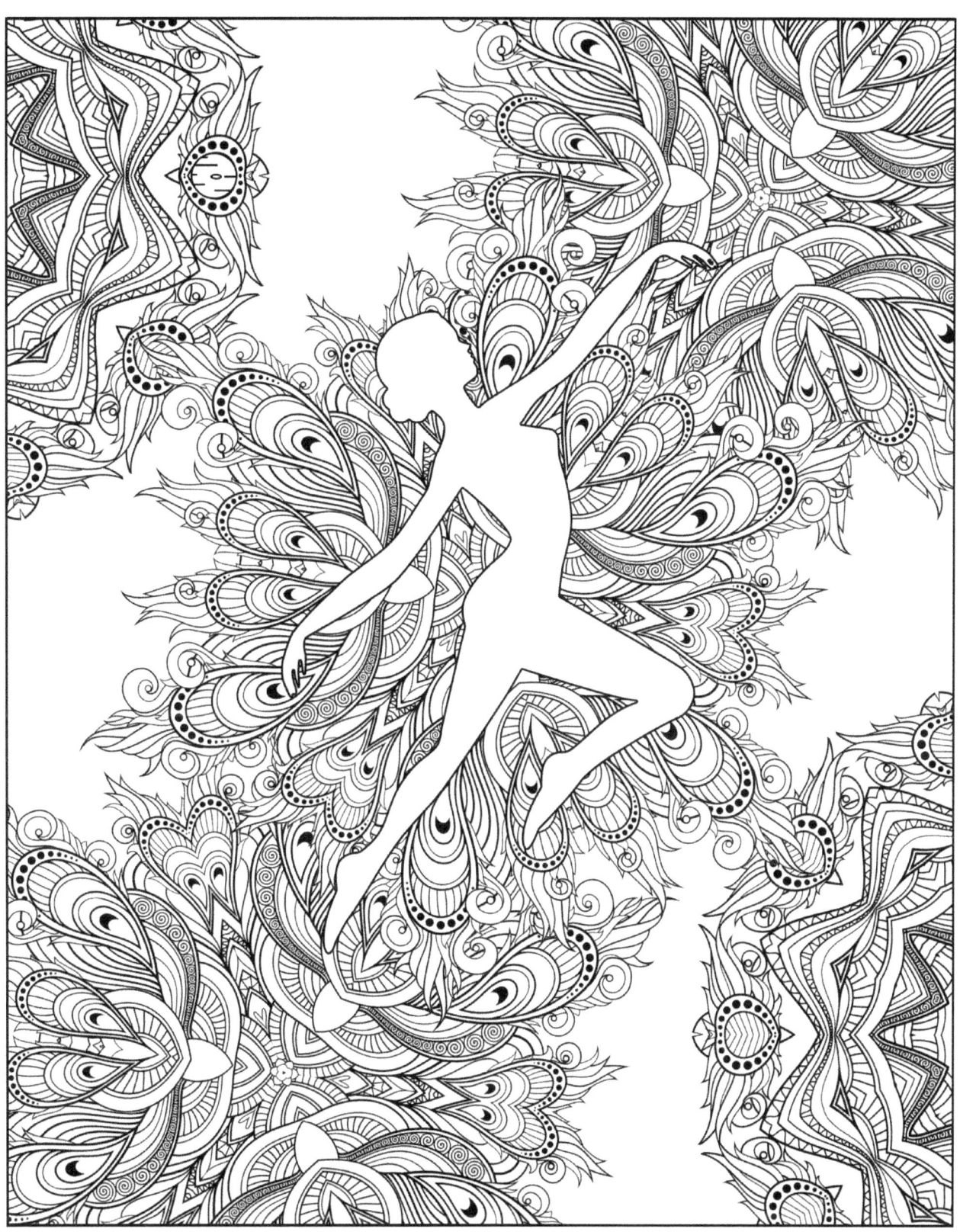

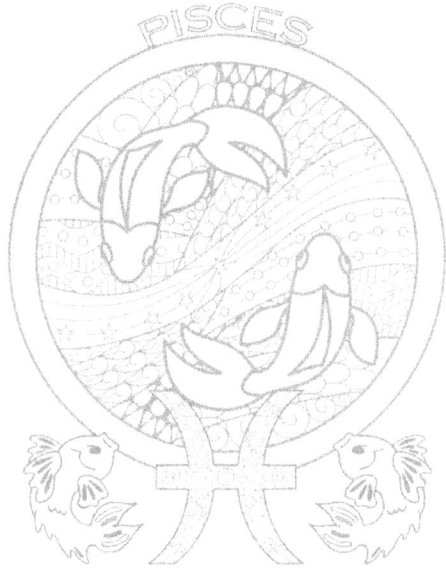

A home on or near the water is wonderful for Pisces.

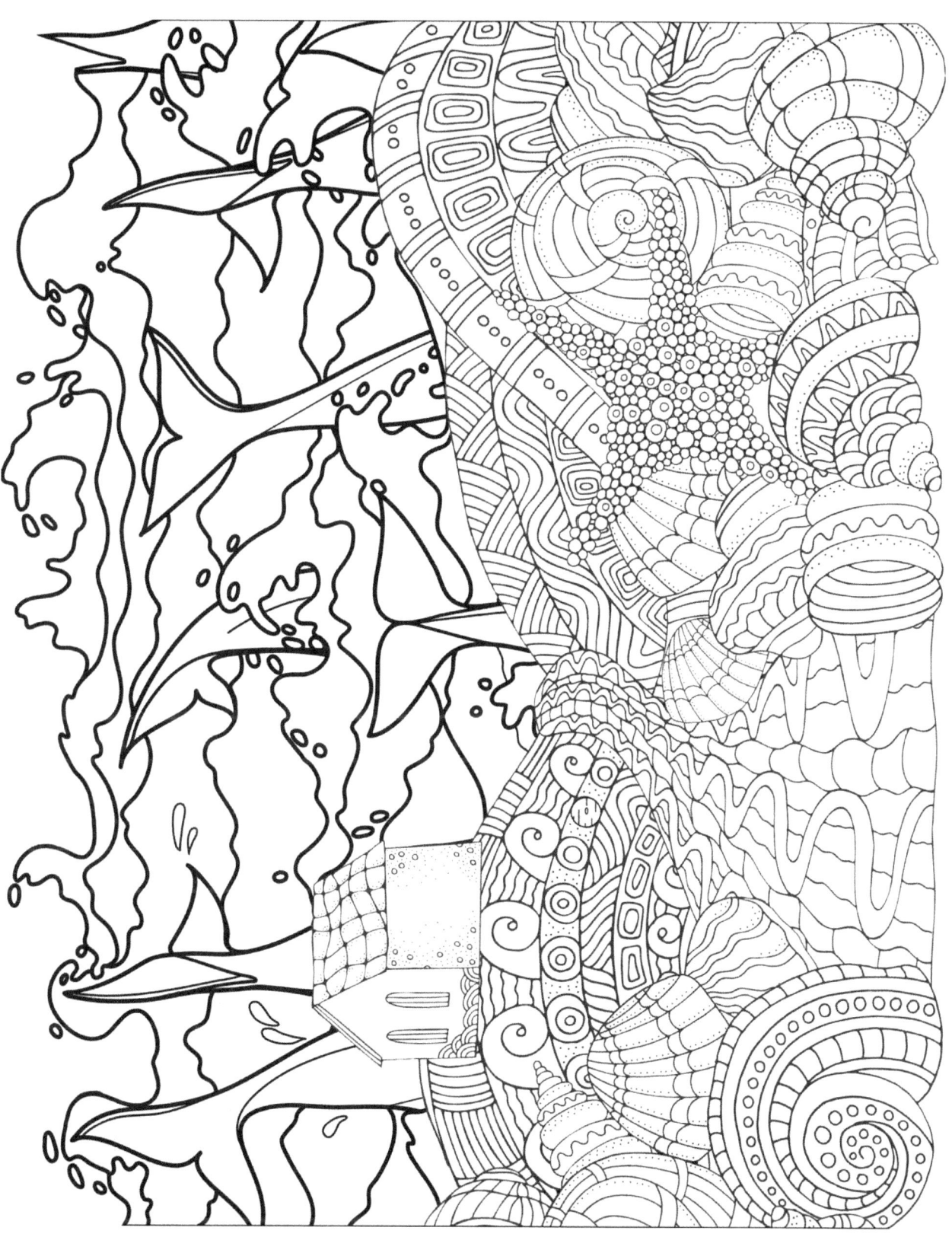

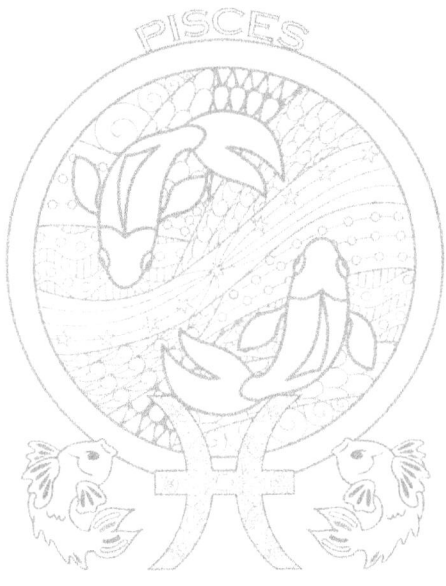

Being highly sensitive and empathetic beings, Pisces may withdraw into themselves to balance and recharge their energy.

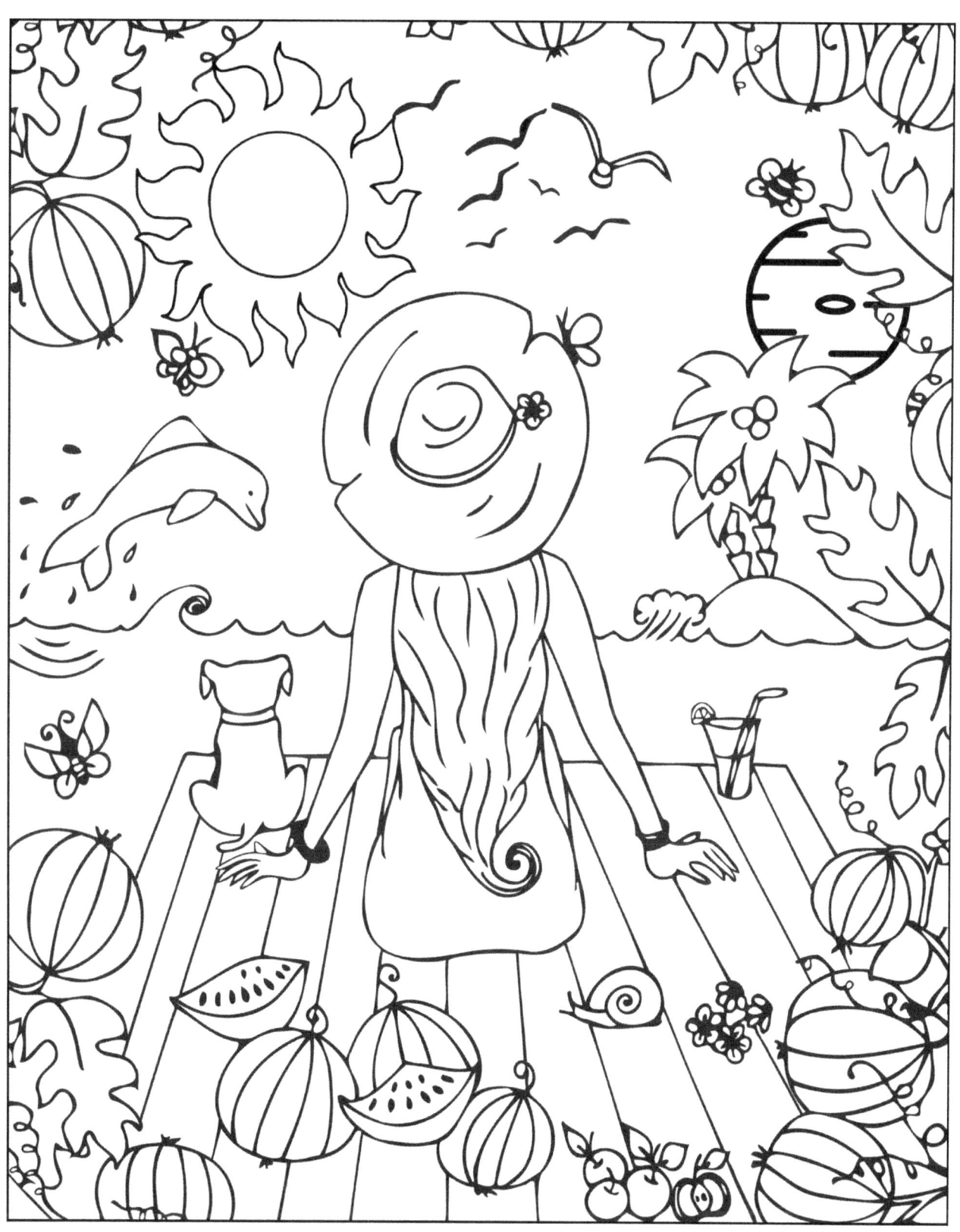

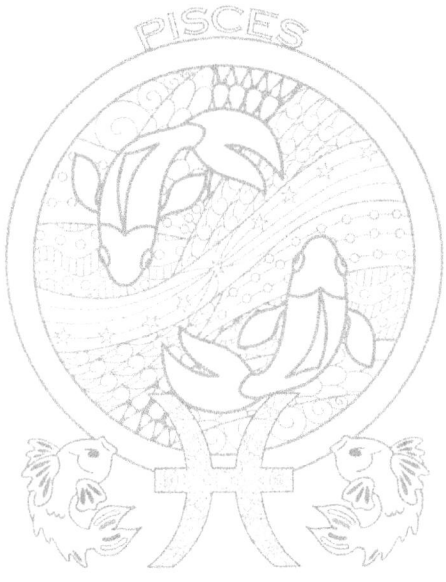

Sailing and boating are wonderful activities for Pisceans.

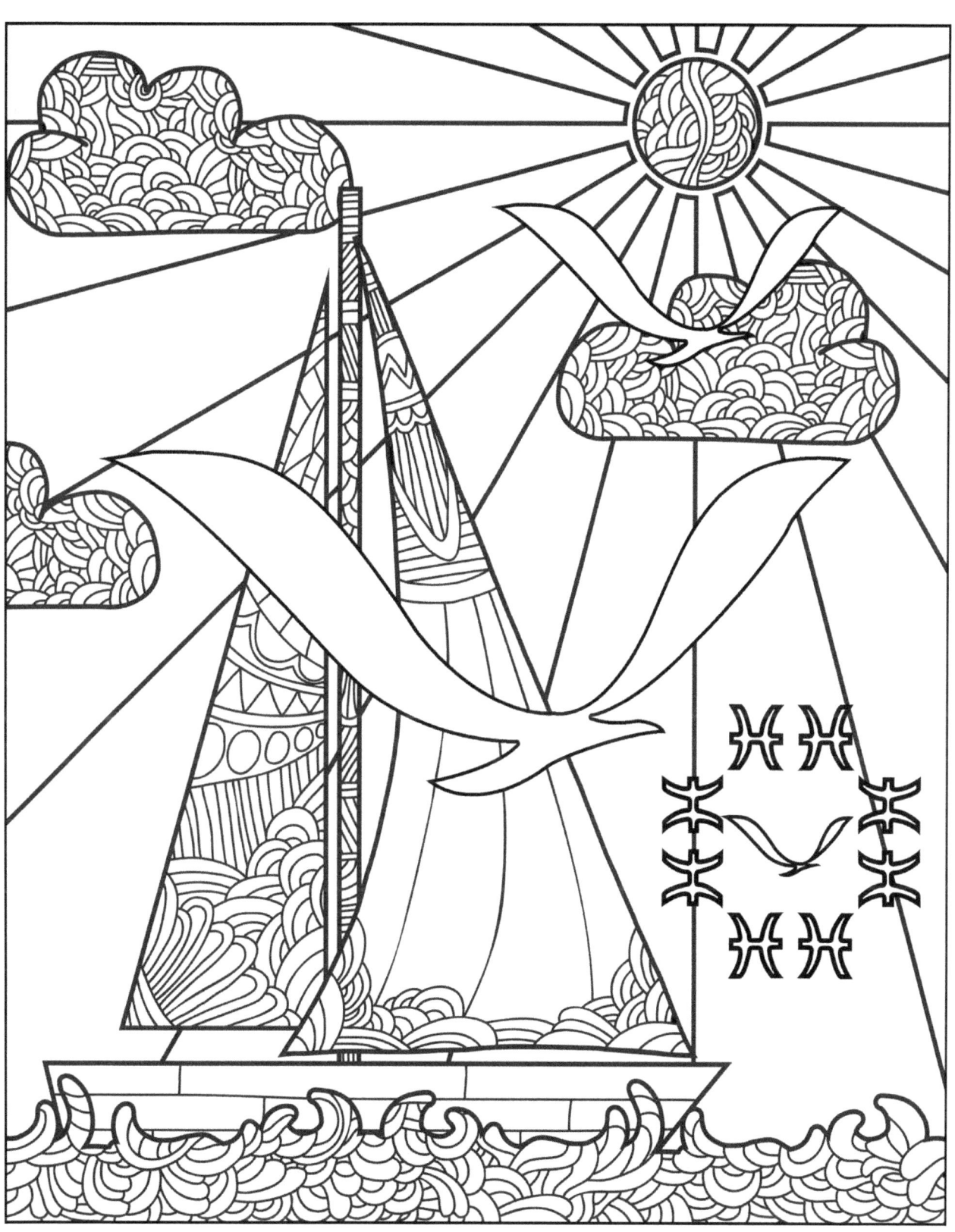

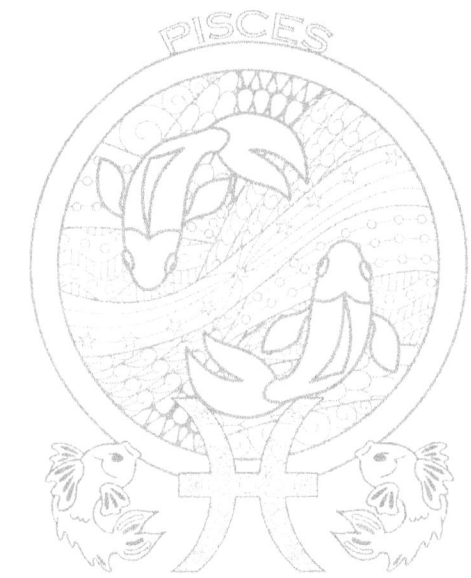

Pisces is symbolized by the image of two fish swimming in different directions which depicts their dual existence with one foot in the ethereal and the other in the earthly world.

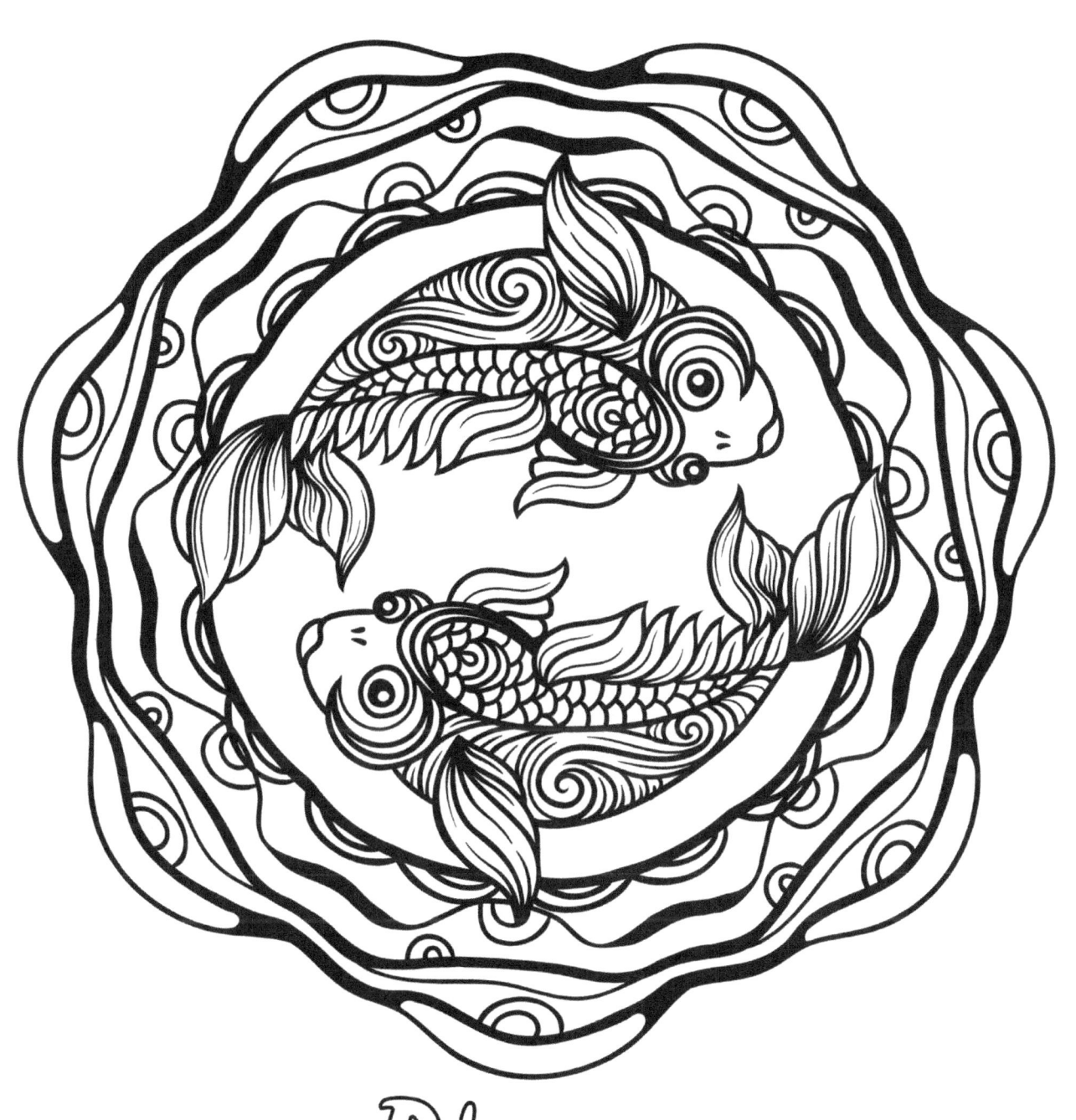

Pisces

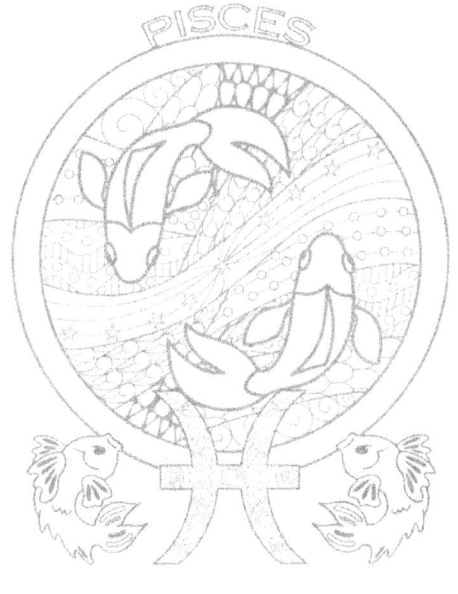

SPECIAL DISCOUNT!

Many customers would like to color some of the coloring pages more than once. If you're one of them we have something special to share with you…

You can get the downloadable pdf version of this book at a special discount because you have purchased this book. You can download the book and print any coloring page as many times as you would like.

To take advantage of this offer simply:

1. Go to the product page:
   https://mytimetocolor.com/piscespdf
2. Add the pdf version to your cart
3. Click on Checkout (cart icon)
4. Enter the coupon code: pdf12zp
5. Complete Checkout
6. Download book and print your favourites!

CONNECT WITH US!

We'd love to connect with you so please visit the website or like us on Facebook!

Website:

www.MyTimeToColor.com

Facebook:

http://Facebook.com/mytimetocolor

POST A REVIEW

Your review means a lot so please consider taking a moment and posting a review where you purchased this book. Thanks!!